Light Many Fires

This book is part of a civic renewal project called Light Many Fires. It is devoted to helping Americans move from political exhaustion toward shared responsibility and constructive engagement.

Light Many Fires offers professionally facilitated, non-partisan dialogues that create space for honest reflection, listening, and connection across differences. These gatherings are provided free of charge as a contribution to the health of our democracy.

To learn more about sponsoring or participating in a dialogue, please visit:

lightmanyfires.org

WHEN
WE THE PEOPLE
LEAD

THE LEADERS WILL FOLLOW

WHEN WE THE PEOPLE LEAD

THE LEADERS WILL FOLLOW

Richard McKnight, PhD

TrueNorth Press

Book: ISBN: 978-0-9824683-8-8
eBook: 978-0-9824683-9-5

Cover and book design: Erin McKnight

Printed in the United States of America.
TrueNorth Press, LLC

FIRST EDITION

To my beloved daughters, whose lives inspire this book:
May your generation lead us toward a freer,
kinder, more resilient America

And to the people of MLUC,
a continual inspiration

A NOTE ON SOURCES

My goal is to give you insights without a lot of academic machinery, while being transparent about my sources, giving credit where it's due. I strive to give credit in the body of the text. Where that is not possible, I've included a section at the back of the book called "Chapter Notes." For readers who simply want to follow the argument, feel free to ignore the Chapter Notes entirely.

CONTENTS

FOREWORD by the Ghost of Thomas Paine   xi

PREFACE   xv

INTRODUCTION A Time That Tries Our Souls   xxi

PART I: HOW WE LOST OUR POWER   1

1   We the Exhausted Majority   3

2   Broken Hearts and Broken Politics   23

3   Of the Rich, By the Rich, For the Rich   47

4   Tyranny of the Minority   67

PART II: RECOVERING OUR POWER   89

5   Subject, Consumer, or Citizen?   91

6   The Inheritors   109

7   Small Numbers, Big Change   125

PART III: LIGHTING THE WAY FORWARD   139

8   Where Do We Go From Here?   141

9   Restoring and Sustaining Democracy   153

10   Light Many Fires   165

EPILOGUE Light Your Fire   181

APPENDIX What the Exhausted Majority Really Believes   183

Notes   187

Acknowledgments   191

Index   193

About the Author   201

FOREWORD

If Thomas Paine were to speak from the beyond, he might say what follows.

My Fellow Americans,

I write to you from beyond the grave with fire in my spectral heart and alarm bells ringing in my soul. The democracy I helped midwife into existence—your democracy—stands threatened. I fear that many of you, distracted by your screens and your algorithms, will fail to stand up as tyrants threaten your country.

I wrote *Common Sense* because the colonists needed to wake up to their power. This book is written for the same reason: because many of you have forgotten that you are the government. You are *not* Subjects waiting for salvation from politicians, you are *not* passive Consumers of it—or shouldn't be. You *are* Citizens with power if you act like it.

The very threats I warned about in 1776 have returned in new dress: tyranny masquerading as patriotism, hypocrites posing as moralists, extremists claiming *they* are the only true patriots, and good people retreating into inaction while demagogues seize control.

You say you love America? You pledge allegiance to America? Then fight for it. Not with muskets but with something far more powerful: civic engagement, acting in numbers with your fellow citizens. The author of this book is correct—when *We the People* lead, the leaders will follow. This was true in my day when we thwarted King George, and it remains true now as you face would-be kings and the bootlickers who aid them.

You are the heirs of a revolution that cast off a crown, that defied the mightiest empire on earth rather than live as subjects. The blood, sacrifice, and courage that won your independence are not relics to be admired from a safe distance, they are a summons to vigilance for all generations. Stand up!

In the midst of your troubles, some of you fantasize about fleeing to other countries or you tune out or become cynical, thinking someone else will fix things. Stop! I didn't risk the hangman's noose so you could abandon the republic when it needed you most. The "Exhausted Majority" described in this book—the nearly 70 percent of you who crave compromise, comity, and common sense—you are the inheritors of everything we fought for. Act like it!

The threats facing you are real: voter suppression, gerrymandering, dark money, the rise of Christian nationalism, nightmare technology that manipulates you, and politicians who prefer ruling to governing. But, from the other side of eternity, here is what should give you hope: Americans have faced worse. Your forebears defeated a powerful King, survived civil war, overcame depression, and vanquished fascism. You can handle some would-be authoritarians if you stop acting like Subjects or Consumers and start acting like Citizens!

This book is not merely an analysis of our troubles; it is a manual for democratic resistance and community involvement. Stand up for democracy. Join something. Volunteer somewhere. Strengthen your communities. Vote in every election. Demand better from your representatives. Refuse to let cynicism become your master.

Each citizen must decide: Will I abandon the very idea of America? Will I bow before cynicism and gloom? Or will I fight like hell, waging the struggle that our very freedom requires? Do not allow despair to have the last word!

With undying faith in you, the people,

Thomas Paine
Eternal Agitator for Liberty

Thomas Paine was not an original signer of the Declaration of Independence but through his book Common Sense, inspired widespread support for the American Revolution throughout the colonies. Published in January 1776, it was America's first bestseller: It sold an estimated 500,000 copies by the end of the Revolution. Adjusted for population, that's the equivalent of tens of millions of copies today.

PREFACE

The TV droned in the background on January 6, 2021, when I heard the words, "They're breaking into the capitol." I turned to watch, my anxiety turning to concern, then worry, then to outrade as I saw American flags being used as weapons against the police. The desecration of the Capitol and the use of the flag as a bludgeon, to me, revealed a crisis not just of politics but of spirit. I found myself fiercely protective of a symbol I didn't realize I had come so much to cherish.

Afterward, and as a consequence, I told a friend that I was going to buy and display an American flag for the first time in my life. He gave me a friendly warning: "Be prepared for some reactions you may not like."

With my wife's blessing, I went to a website to buy the flag, and I read this in the product description:

PROUDLY DISPLAY YOUR PATRIOTIC FEELINGS:

Express your love and your admiration for this great country!

Though committed to the purchase, I was taken aback by the word "patriotic." I stopped and asked myself: *Am* I patriotic? I do love the convictions on which this country was founded, but do I truly love my discord-riven, deeply flawed country?

After putting out the flag, I got one of those reactions my friend warned me about shortly after, not from the guy whose faded Trump/Pence sign from 2016 had finally fallen from the tree in his yard, but from my neighbor, an outspoken Democrat. Approaching me on the sidewalk one day, he asked reproachfully, "Are you a Trump supporter?" When I said no, he said, "Your flag tells me your home is a MAGA enclave."

My reply was quick and clear: I see Donald Trump's influence as deeply damaging to our democratic norms, but I hardly believe that all Republicans share his values. I said that many Republicans still hold fast to principles on which our country was founded, have integrity, and offer service to their communities. With those people, I am proud to be associated.

Sometime later, I wrote an editorial about the flag and why Democrats (like me) should fly it just as many Republicans do. Based on this, I was asked to give a talk to a group of liberals. In my remarks, I urged my audience to reclaim our symbol, asserting that doing so would potentially rekindle a spirit of enthusiasm for our country—at least in them. Afterward, most people thanked me, and some later sent photos of their own flags. But a small number objected. One said their anger at the country's failings ran so deep that they would never consider flying the flag. Another was openly seething: "I hate this country. If I had the means, I'd move to another country tomorrow."

This broke my heart. When people of conscience retreat from our nation's symbol—not to mention moving away from the country itself—we allow others who don't have our interests at heart to define and determine it.

As I've been writing this book, I've spoken to many people about my growing faith in America. One friend who has known me since my hippie days could hardly believe his ears. "Aren't you the guy that marched against the Vietnam War?" Another said, "How did you become such a Pollyanna?" Another hastened to point out our country's flaws. I am very happy to say, though, that 95 percent of the people who heard about this book still believe in our country's potential and not only wished me well but offered to help by telling me stories and in other ways, too. You will meet some of them in these pages.

To the naysayers, I get it. Ours is the story of an imperfect people trying to live up to some lofty ideals. We're blemished and defective. We do terrible things at times. And now, it seems we've completely lost our way. But as I have come to understand our history, I see us as a people who make mistakes but who also learn from them, who prevail, who strive and get better. And who are deeply good.

If you're young, you're probably cynical about America right now. I was once deeply cynical myself, especially during the Vietnam War, when it seemed like the country had abandoned its own principles, and again later during the Iraq War. Both periods left a mark on me. But they also taught me something important: Cynicism is a natural response to betrayal, but it's not a sustainable way to live. Eventually, you either give up or start looking for places where ordinary people are doing the slow work of repairing what's broken. I chose the latter. I hope you will, too.

In contemplating the events of January 6, I have come to recognize that when people lose faith in the transcendent purpose that democracy had once provided and when religion falters or becomes divisive, something else must fill the void. If that "something" is fear, resentment, or, in the case of Christian nationalism, the hunger for domination, democracy cannot survive—unless the rest of us maintain the faith.

If each of us carries the faith that our neighbors are capable of goodness, that our shared life has meaning, that justice is real, then democracy can heal itself from within.

Looked at in this light, January 6 was not just a political riot—it revealed a profound collapse of faith in one another. It was a moment when part of the nation, untethered from truth and trust, attempted to seize by force what can only be sustained by mutual faith. I do not mean this in a religious sense. I mean that the only antidote to despair in a people like ours is not cynicism or counter-rage but the recovery of belief in one another's basic goodness and a belief that the ideals symbolized by the flag are still worth nurturing—and can again light our darkness.

With this book I aim to play Cupid and attract you, perhaps for the first time, to your country and its potential. Another is to convince you there are meaningful answers to the question, "What can I do that could possibly make any kind of a difference?" Further, I am going to claim that as you join with others to restore our country, you will be happier and more likely to flourish.

I had my 78th birthday while writing this book. I've lived through enough American seasons to recognize when we're at an inflection point. This book is my attempt to offer you a perspective that might help you build an America you can be proud of. You certainly don't need an old man to tell you what to think, but what I can offer is a long view as to how change happens, how faith ebbs and returns, and how much power ordinary people have when they act together.

People, let's do this.

INTRODUCTION

A Time That Tries Our Souls

Americans are told, over and over again, that we are a people at war with one another. The fancy word is polarization. We are repeatedly told we're divided, hostile, that are differences are irreconcilable. But I will prove that this story is a big fat lie. Someone profits from telling us this lie. I will tell you who that is. All of us must push back on the lie. Our mental health depends on it, and our liberty does, too.

Though we may not be at war with one another, most of us are not happy with how conflict is handled and the way our politics go. Some of us are so disgusted with our country we're leaving or considering leaving. Most of us, even if we have no thought of leaving our country, feel a deep unease about it and look away. It's a relationship that, for many of us, is breaking down.

I spent over forty years as a social psychologist, helping people and organizations mend fractured relationships. Again and again, I saw this: When a relationship reaches a breaking point, we face three possible paths. Today, with respect to the relationship we have with our troubled nation, each of us must choose which one to take.

Leave it. This choice seems to have special appeal for liberals, the fallen idealists of our time. This choice also appeals to the roughly 26 percent of Americans who have opted out of political life entirely, the group researchers call "the Disengaged." Most concerning, this option tempts many young people, the very generation that will inherit the future.

Break it. This is the path of political warfare, of treating opponents as enemies to be eliminated. A very powerful minority on the right is doing this, including Donald Trump and his ilk. Steve Bannon uses this very language: Burn the whole system down, he says.

Stand up for it. This is the hardest path. It's the choice to work with others to repair what's broken. It asks us to face some uncomfortable truths: America is far from perfect, no one is coming to save us, and none of us alone can bring it closer to its promise. Yet each of us, in concert with others, can restore the integrity of our system and make our community lives better and richer.

This book is filled with stories of people, heroic and everyday, who are doing exactly that. These are ordinary Americans who have decided not to walk away, not to give in, but to stand up for the country they still believe can be better, by *making* it better.

If standing up for America is the choice you're making, even if this is something you're considering, this book is for you. Speaking personally, I am not going to leave or break something. No one takes my country and my liberty from me. I am in this for the long haul. And I am going to try to convince you to be, too.

Even if you are ambivalent about our country, I want to entice you to become intimate with our country, to understand its founding aspirations more deeply as well as the problems it faces, and then to join with others to improve it. I am hopeful that what you read here will help you find a way to take your fear, or anger, or whatever you're feeling about our country, and find a way to help America get back on track. We've done it before and we can do it again.

An American tradition and the actual defining characteristic of democracy is that *We the People* can effect change when it's necessary. In fact, no one else can. Yes, the people who make laws and oversee the function of our government have power. In our system, *We the People* give it to them. And our history tells us that when sweeping change occurs, it's because *We the People* made our lawmakers do the legal work required.

Time and again, when Americans have organized, persisted, and made their voices heard loudly enough, politicians have responded. *We the People* have forced politicians to pass laws protecting workers and giving them the right to organize. *We the People* caused an end to the Vietnam war, the elimination of laws preventing interracial marriage, and the legalization of same-sex marriage, and on, and on, and on. Women's rights. Jim Crow laws. On and on.

Of course, this is easy to say. When things aren't working, and when we're socially isolated from one another, it can be hard to know what to do or how to begin advocating for the things that matter to us. Following the talks I've given on the themes in this book, the most common question I hear is, "What could *I* possibly do? I'm just little ol' me." One of my aims in writing this book is to help you answer that question.

To this point, at the end of every chapter you will find a short section called "Stepping Into Your Power." These sections contain thoughts about influence, politics, and how one person, by shifting the way they think about their own daily conduct, can acquire greater agency.

You may not feel powerful right now. That's understandable; many of us don't. The problems around us are big, and there are few inspiring leaders showing us how to be effective together. But you *do* have power. You use it every day in how you speak up, what you support, what you avoid, and whom you stand with, and you can add your power to the many existing initiatives to improve our country. As you do this, you will feel more confident of the future because you're helping to build it.

In a sea of social media that foments despair, three dark forces threaten democracy.

This isn't about doing something dramatic. It's about learning to see yourself differently: not as a spectator of our government, or as a consumer of it, but as a citizen with a place in making our government and way of life work. One small step, taken with intention, is all you need to begin.

Now, let me introduce the hard part of this book, the powerful forces that swirl together and create our present troubles. This whirlwind is depicted in the graphic (previous page). Political extremism, civic decline, and oligarchic wealth are what ail us. Together, these forces create what I think of as a spiritual crisis, in the middle of the graphic. Surrounding, suffusing, and accelerating all three of those forces is social media.

If you have a pulse and don't live under a rock, you're probably troubled by what's happening in our country. Very large numbers of Americans are. Anxiety is common among us; so is fear. Many of us fear financial ruin, others political violence, still others a dystopian future or civil war. This is the center of the whirlwind, the despair we feel. Many of us—older, better resourced, supported by family—can withstand the current storm. But countless others cannot and are being battered cruelly.

I use the term *spiritual crisis* for this constellation of troubles because it captures not just the symptoms but the deeper ache beneath them. Maybe the term spiritual crisis makes you uncomfortable. If so, substitute the term "mental health crisis" or "existential crisis" instead, but even these terms tell of the depth of the problem we face. I'll explore this crisis more fully in Chapter Two.

When I use the term political extremism in the preceding graphic, I am referring to a menacing minority on the extreme right that pretends to be about preserving what's essential about our nation but that is actually intent on degrading our liberty and recasting our country as a theocracy, a government grounded in a state religion. This movement goes by several names—Christian nationalism, MAGA, national conservatism. It is the focus of Chapter Four.

The extremism I'm describing thrives in the vacuum left by civic decline, the collapse of everyday participation in community life. Fewer of us now vote, volunteer, or spend time in the places that once connected neighbors and built trust: churches, service clubs, union halls, and local meetings. Without that trust, more people become vulnerable to the appeals of extremism. As I'll show in Chapter Two, civic engagement has been falling for decades. But the good news is, it can be rebuilt; we've done this before.

The third force, oligarchy, is the subject of Chapter Three. This is an economic system in which a very small number of extremely wealthy people control the politics, economics, and media of a nation. Such a system concentrates wealth in the hands of a few. In such a system, *We the People* have less and less power. Because we value our liberty, we must curb this system.

All of these problems, while dire, can be addressed if we work smart and work together. Through this book, I hope to enlist you in the emerging movement that seeks to refresh our democracy and ensure the conditions in which it thrives.

Here's the good news: What this requires from each of us has very positive *personal* payoffs; it's a win-win. When we take action on behalf of the greater good, it's good for democracy, and it's good for our own health and happiness. The truth is when we do *anything* to build community—reaching out to a neighbor who needs help, volunteering for an hour at the library, or even starting a club—personal stress goes down. We lower our stress when we add something to our community by creating or joining a block association, shoveling the sidewalk of a neighbor, coaching a little league team, or volunteering for something. Even joining a book club lowers stress. And importantly, we lower our stress when we refuse to believe our fellow citizens are our enemies.

In this book, while I encourage you to devote time to the betterment of your neighborhood, your community, and your country, I urge you to do so through actions that respect your time, your energy, and commitments. You don't have to become a political activist or devote your life to a cause to play a meaningful role in helping our country get back on track. Standing up for your country should start with standing up for your neighborhood and your community.

Join With Others

That phrase is the key to the political and social turnaround we need. Even more important than our relationship with our country is our relationship, as citizens, with one another. We need one another and our country needs us: to work together, to join together. As *We the People* work together, we become powerful. As *We the People* stand up, the elected leaders notice and respond. They always have.

WHEN *WE THE PEOPLE* LEAD, THE LEADERS WILL FOLLOW

This is not just a clever phrase; it's a fact supported by history and by research, as we'll discover. When even a sliver of the population shows up steadily and refuses to relent, political leaders will take the steps necessary to defend democratic life. Americans in every era must preserve and renew democracy. Ours is no different.

This book follows the arc of a journey we must take in our time.

Part I puts us on a hard road. In it, we examine how we've been shaped into spectators and subjects and moved away from the citizen role. Part I asks us to face the forces that have drained our confidence, frayed our trust, and left so many feeling dispirited. James Baldwin once said, "Not everything that is faced can be changed, but nothing can be changed until it is faced." Naming these realities is the first act of liberation. My hope is that by confronting the spell we're under, we begin to understand why we feel so overwhelmed.

In Part II, we learn to travel not as individuals but as fellow citizens, building strength in company with others. This enables us to understand the core task of every American today: To say no to being a subject and to reclaim our power, to move away from the stupefying consumer mentality. This is the work of rediscovering the habits, mindsets, and alliances that make citizenship revitalizing and uplifting. Along this road, we remember that democracy isn't a machine that runs by itself; it's a *practice* that depends on citizens regularly exhibiting the routines of care for one another.

Having faced what is broken and with our tools of courage and cooperation in hand, we now act, repairing institutions and rebuilding community. In Part III, we make the choices that enable us to continue the journey and to do the work that renewal requires. The journey does not end at the crossroads; it begins there.

PART I
How We Lost
Our Power

Every democracy in history has had moments when its people grew tired of shouting, of losing faith, of wondering if anything they can do will improve things. *We the People* are living through one of those moments. The headlines scream polarization, but beneath the noise lies something quieter and even more dangerous for democracy: exhaustion.

This section begins by naming that exhaustion. The intent is not to wallow but to see it so we can put something more wholesome in its place. Only by facing the truth of our weariness can we recover the will to act. We will meet the "Exhausted Majority," the bulk of Americans who want decency and compromise but feel—and are—sidelined and worn out.

We will confront the sad state of civic engagement in our country today and how democracy suffers for it. We will look inward at the heartbreak beneath our politics: the loss of community, purpose, and friendship; the erosion of trust that has left so many feeling alone and discouraged about our country.

We will learn about how a determined minority of political extremists has brought about a "tyranny of the minority" and how this group is trying to weaponize citizen apathy and anger to redefine what America is.

We will also learn how a very small number of extremely wealthy Americans are increasingly controlling the tax laws, government regulation of industry, and the flow of information that shapes what citizens believe, discuss, see on their screens, vote for, and even think.

Part I is the act in which the hero faces the dragon and admits fear. Naming what's broken is the first act of repair. When we look unflinchingly at what's wrong, we become clearer about what we need to put back in place.

1

We are in a fight not against each
other, but against the forces that
thrive on chaos and division and are
willing to destroy our institutions
for the sake of power.

—ADAM KINZINGER, FORMER
CONGRESSMAN

We are the ones we have been
waiting for.

—JUNE JORDAN, AFRICAN
AMERICAN POET AND ACTIVIST

We the Exhausted Majority

*Who We Are, What We Want,
Why We've Been Sidelined*

Maybe you know someone like Ashley, a 43 year-old woman I spoke to while writing this book. Maybe you *are* someone
like Ashley. This is pretty likely since Ashley's views and behaviors are typical of a very large percentage of Americans.

Ashley works in a marketing role at a healthcare system in
a suburb of a midwestern city. She was raised a Methodist but

stopped going to church during college. She is worried about our country as many of us are. "I wonder if we're going to have another Civil War," she said.

To Ashley, politics feels like a toxic game, one she never wanted to play. She told me she cares about fairness and decency, but politics to her feels like a shouting match between people who don't know how to listen. She told me she thinks she "should probably care more about politics" but is largely disengaged. She votes some years, skips others, and feels vaguely guilty that she's not doing what a citizen should, although when I asked her what they would look like, she wasn't sure.

When I spoke with Ashley, a working mother, she said, "It feels like everything's broken and I'm not sure anyone's even trying to fix it. All politicians do is shout."

Does she pay attention to current events, I asked? "I scroll through the headlines but not every day. It mostly makes me feel tired," she told me. To assess how well informed she is, I asked if she could name three Supreme Court Justices. She could not. Does she know the names of the Senators from her state? She could name one but not the other.

Ashley could not speak about politics without revealing strong feelings, but those emotions pointed nowhere in particular. "Why do politicians fight with one another all the time?" she asked, offering the view that "They are all corrupt, both Republicans and Democrats. They only care about themselves." That brought up the question: Is she a Democrat or a Republican? "I'm registered as a Democrat, but I'm really an independent," she said. Both parties feel disappointing to her, more interested in bickering than solving problems.

Ashley worries about the high cost of living, climate change and healthcare costs but thinks her voice and views mean nothing to those in power. By turns, she was annoyed, anxious, and disillusioned with anything relating to government. She came off as a victim of politics and government, utterly without agency.

I asked about her involvement in her community. "I don't go to church, but I give to the Salvation Army at Christmas," she said. Is she a member of a club or service organization? "Not currently." Why not? "Work and family keep me very busy."

Ashley wants harmony in America, but her confusion keeps her on the sidelines. She doesn't see an "enemy" or "opponent" so much as a fog of dysfunction. This leaves her without urgency, and thus, she takes no action. I told her about this book. Does she think she would read something that might help her find ways to work with others to reclaim our politics and create more community feeling?

"Honestly?" she said. "Probably not. Just thinking about things like that makes me really nervous."

Maybe you aren't like Ashley. Maybe you're more like Tony, a 52-year-old manager at an electrical contracting business who lives in a suburb north of Philadelphia. He is a born-again Christian. He watches Fox News almost exclusively. I asked him about his religious beliefs and how they show up in his life, how they shape his perspective on America. He was remarkably open and very articulate.

How knowledgeable is Tony about our government? Where Ashley could name only one Supreme Court Justice, Tony named all nine. He called the so-called liberal judges "the communist left-wing of the court." He named both of Pennsylvania's senators.

Tony believes that both America and his religious faith are under siege. From his vantage point, his faith is mocked in schools and families are undermined by atheists in Hollywood and other cultural institutions. He thinks America is in a state of moral collapse. All of this leaves him feeling alarmed, on guard, and convinced that if people like him don't "return our country to its Christian roots," it will be no more.

Throughout our conversation, Tony used the language of war. He used the term "fight" and "fighting" repeatedly. He spoke of "enemies" without hesitation, referring to other Americans. He said people like him are trying to "kill" dangerous beliefs and corrupting lifestyles. For him, the enemies are secular progressives, globalists, transvestites, and those who, in his view, reject God's plan for humanity and the United States.

When Tony sits in his church for up to three services and prayer meetings each week, he feels part of an army. When he goes to the polls, he knows he's part of a powerful, coordinated movement. His pastor tells him that every election is a battlefield, every vote a weapon. The Voter Guides provided by the Faith & Freedom Coalition through his church confirm his choice of whom to vote for. For Tony, the stakes of politics are eternal. His clarity and affiliation give him energy and purpose.

If you value living in a country in which no single faith or faction dominates, where all people have equal rights and a fair say in public life, the contrast between Tony and Ashley, stand-ins for sizable groups of Americans, should make you worry.

Between Ashley and Tony lies the fault line that defines this era of our democracy: an exhausted majority on one side that is turning away from involvement in our politics and community life and a fervent minority on the other. Ashley's quiet weariness is far more representative of the country than Tony's certainty. And that lethargy, if we can learn from it, may yet become the beginning of renewal.

Researchers have a name for the population that Ashley belongs to: *the Exhausted Majority.* The phrase comes from the Hidden Tribes study, which found that nearly two-thirds of Americans share her outlook: frustrated by the noise, yearning for compromise, and unwilling to see neighbors as enemies.[1]

Make no mistake: There *is* polarization in America, especially in the run-up to elections and when research subjects are asked for their party affiliation before they give their opinions. Yet research shows the majority of us do not think principally of ourselves in political terms and are *not* polarized. Ashley isn't, but Tony is. Ashley is at war with no one. Tony is at war with anyone who is "woke."

Even though we're constantly told we despise one another, the research tells a different story. Many studies show that most Americans simply want things to get better. They're weary of the shouting, the outrage, and the performative politics that make our public life feel more like a wrestling match than a republic. They want change, but many don't know where to begin or how to make their efforts matter.

If most Americans aren't polarized, what terms describe us more accurately? How about this: Most Americans make up the broad, steady majority that keeps this country running in the everyday ways that matter most. They are the quiet strength of our communities. These are the people who, despite all the noise, still believe that decency, dialogue, and compromise can solve problems.

If you're like these Americans—and you probably are—you have friends and relatives across the political spectrum, and your conversations with them are mostly civil, respectful, even caring. You believe in the possibility of America's renewal, yet you worry that the nation is coming apart. You may be weary of politics, but deep down you still trust that this country can do better, even if the path forward is not yet clear.

That's why the constant conflict and outrage in the news feels so alien and so exhausting. Research confirms what you already sense in your bones: Americans share far more in common than what divides us.

SEVEN TRIBES

The Hidden Tribes research found that, based on values and perspectives on issues of the day, Americans fall into seven groups or "tribes." As we go along, you might want to find your "tribe."

The Exhausted Majority includes people slightly left of center, those in the middle, and those slightly right of center. This is not where the polarization lies; it exists between the smaller tribes on the left and right, the so-called "wings."

Those in the Exhausted Majority are far less likely than those on the ideological wings to define themselves in political terms. They worry more about the country's deepening divisions than about advancing any particular ideology. Survey after survey shows that large majorities within this group—often 70 percent or more—believe the media exaggerates our conflicts and that Americans share far more common ground than we're led to think.

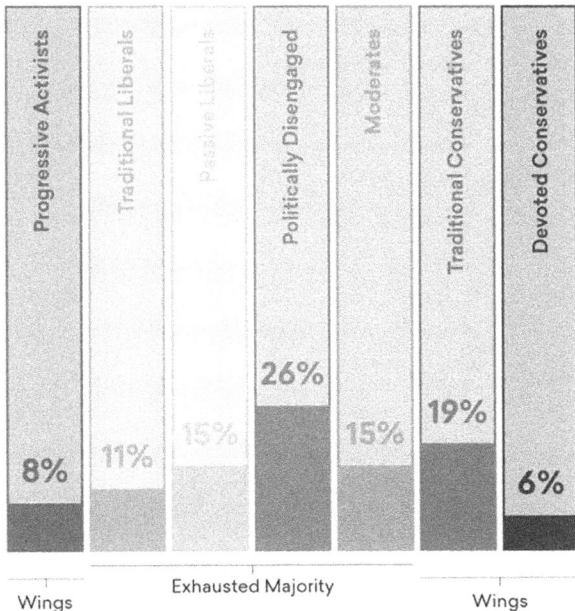

Progressive Activists — 8%
Traditional Liberals — 11%
Passive Liberals — 15%
Politically Disengaged — 26%
Moderates — 15%
Traditional Conservatives — 19%
Devoted Conservatives — 6%

Wings | Exhausted Majority | Wings

Source: *Hidden Tribes: A Study of America's Polarized Landscape* (More in Common, 2018). Used with permission.

In short, they are not disengaged because they don't care. They are disengaged because they are disheartened. They are worn down by the tone, the rancor, and the performative politics that now pass for public life.

These findings have been independently verified by other researchers including Kristen Soltis Anderson, a Republican pollster. In summarizing a year's worth of focus groups, she wrote:

It turns out we don't want a tyranny of one side over the other, but the decency of compromise. We don't want purity tests or culture war crusades, but practical steps that improve daily life. We want representatives and a President who remember that their job is to serve the citizens, not the political class or their cronies and not the top one percent of earners. We want a country where neighbors can differ without hatred, and where the republic is renewed, not consumed, by debate.[2]

Further, these findings echo the work of political scientists at Stanford. Their research presents two curves: one showing who Americans actually are on a range of issues and another showing who we *think* Americans are. If we were truly a highly polarized nation, the distribution of political views would resemble the curve on the left—heavy at the extremes, with very few people in the middle. But that's not what the data show.[3]

<table>
<tr><td align="center">We think most people's
views are at the extremes.</td><td align="center">People's views are more
alike than different.</td></tr>
</table>

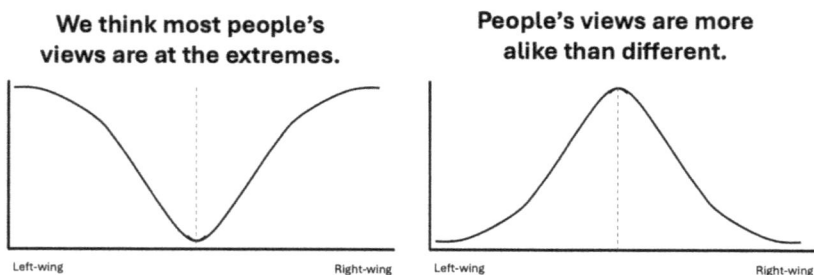

Left-wing   Right-wing   Left-wing   Right-wing

On a host of issues, Americans, even across so-called "red" states and "blue" states, agree on many issues. The actual distribution looks more like the curve on the right.

The authors of the Stanford study state:

There is little evidence that Americans' ideological or policy positions are more polarized today than they were two or three decades ago, although their choices [in elections] often seem to be. The explanation is that the political figures Americans evaluate [when they vote] are more polarized. A polarized political class makes the citizenry appear polarized, but it is only that—an appearance.

The Stanford researchers also answer the question: *If we aren't polarized, why do we seem to be*? One answer is "because political party activists themselves convince us that we are." As they put it, the politicians at the extremes—far-right and far-left—"hate each other and regard themselves as combatants in a war."

Unlike those on the far-right and -left, the Hidden Tribes researchers found that those in the Exhausted Majority support finding political compromise (65 percent) and believe that the nation needs to heal (64 percent). People in this group consistently identify America's political divisions as a primary concern.

If you are in the Exhausted Majority, you feel forgotten in the political debate—and you are!

THE SEVEN HIDDEN TRIBES OF AMERICAN POLITICAL CULTURE

Progressive Activists (8%)
Highly engaged, left-leaning, deeply concerned about inequality, discrimination, and climate change. See activism and protest as key tools for change and often distrust traditional institutions.

Traditional Liberals (11%)
Classic, open-minded liberals. Value tolerance, diversity, and reasoned debate. Less confrontational than Progressive Activists and more willing to work across political lines.

Passive Liberals (15%)
Lean liberal but less politically active. Dislike conflict and polarization, feel politically homeless, and often withdraw from public debate even though they care about fairness and compassion.

The Politically Disengaged (26%)
The largest group, often young or economically strained. They rarely vote or follow politics and feel powerless to influence events. Tend to see the system as rigged or irrelevant to their lives.

Moderates (15%)
Pragmatic, middle-of-the-road. Value compromise and civility. Dislike extremes on both sides and are motivated more by common-sense solutions than ideology.

Traditional Conservatives (19%)
Patriotic, religious, and institution-respecting Americans who emphasize personal responsibility, family, faith, and community. Value stability and civility over disruption.

Devoted Conservatives (6%)
Ideologically very consistent and politically active. See moral decay everywhere and threats to traditional values. Believe their way of life must be defended vigorously, sometimes viewing compromise as weakness.

BROAD IDEOLOGICAL AGREEMENT

Not only are those of us in the Exhausted Majority not deeply divided, but it also turns out that we substantially agree on a long list of issues, including abortion, gun control, and money in politics.

Across a wide range of issues, Americans in the Exhausted Majority share strikingly similar views. This group overwhelmingly supports universal background checks on guns, raising the purchase age to 21, investing in infrastructure, job retraining, affordable childcare, and a higher minimum wage. Most also favor curbing the influence of money in politics and other electoral reforms, and oppose the *Citizens United* ruling.

On social issues, around two-thirds of those in the Exhausted Majority support legal abortion in most or all cases. Further, large majorities (83 percent–96 percent) say racism is a serious problem, 82 percent believe it is common, and 68 percent see white supremacy as a growing threat.

Agreement areas extend also to same-sex marriage (64 percent), acceptance of transgender people as morally right (66 percent), and though many fault Biden for mismanagement of immigration, most say immigration benefits the nation (60 percent). (For a more complete list, see Appendix: *What the Exhausted Majority Really Believes.*)

The Hidden Tribes study did find that while we all may not be at one another's throats, some Americans do have "absurdly inaccurate perceptions of each other." For example, when Republicans in this study were asked what Democrats believe, they were way off, but Democrats are even worse in understanding what Republicans believe on key issues.

Other research confirms this pattern. The *Perception Gap* study (conducted by Hidden Tribes, the same research group) found that when Democrats were asked what percentage of Republicans believe that "properly controlled immigration can be good for America," they were off by over 50 percent: Respondents guessed only 48 percent would agree; in reality, nearly 80 percent of Republicans agreed.

Intriguingly, greater education and deeper political engagement do not necessarily foster empathy for those on the other side; in many cases, this appears to do the opposite: Highly educated progressives who closely follow the news are often among the least accurate in understanding what their political opponents actually believe. The pattern is not limited to the left. Those on the far right—the Traditional and Devoted Conservatives—tend to misperceive others just as badly. In short, the more politically immersed people are at the extremes, the more distorted their perceptions of fellow Americans can become. (If you'd like to assess how well *you* know people who vote under different banners than you, take the five-minute quiz at perceptiongap.us.)

THE EXHAUSTED MAJORITY HAS BEEN SIDELINED

The Hidden Tribes research found that most of us in the Exhausted Majority feel disempowered by and unrepresented in our political system. A large majority of the Exhausted Majority agreed that "politicians don't care about people like them." They also expressed feeling "forgotten in the political debate." This disempowerment is rooted in the feeling that they "do not feel their voice can make a difference."

Many of us feel completely invisible in *local* politics, let alone at the *federal* level. That sense of alienation turns into passivity and disengagement, both dangerous in a system of self-government. According to the Hidden Tribes report, members of the Exhausted Majority are far less politically active than the "wing" tribes. This disengagement isn't simply nonparticipation; it reflects a deeper withdrawal from the kind of public conversation that shapes our country. The report says, "almost half the members of the Exhausted Majority select 'none' when asked to select ways they have been active politically in the past year." The list included sharing content, donating, attending meetings, and other activities.

The Exhausted Majority is also sidelined because various structural mechanisms built into the voting and election process promote disengagement and reward extremism. I'm referring here to partisan gerrymandering, closed party primaries that empower the most ideologically motivated voters, the flood of money from interest groups and super Political Action Committees (PACs), and the winner-take-all system that discourages independent or centrist voices. To address this, some states are moving to ranked choice voting; if your first choice can't win, your vote goes to your next choice until someone has a majority. This weeds out extreme candidates, but some, especially on the far-right, resist this.

Many of us feel that our needs and interests are of no consequence to most politicians, and quite often, we're correct: A major study into the impact of ordinary voters in determining public policy recently concluded that "the preferences of the average American appear to have only a minuscule, *near-zero*, statistically non-significant impact upon public policy [my italics]." This research also found that public opinion from the bottom 90 percent of income earners has essentially *no* impact on policy outcomes, while economic elites and organized interest groups hold substantial influence.[4]

We may feel overlooked and lack clout overall, but, as we'll see, voters in the Exhausted Majority have already shaped key elections and can be a powerful force going forward, if we act together.

MEDIA SEPARATES US

Another reason we're sidelined lies in the negative impact of social media that separates us into echo chambers and keeps us off balance and misinformed. Increasingly, media creates outrage. As pundit Scott Galloway said, "We used to think sex sells. What we found is something better, and that is rage."

This brings up the question: *Who profits from outrage, whether real or perceived?* The Hidden Tribes researchers noted that there is big money in polarization; it's the fuel that keeps social media, cable news, and talk radio running. As political maps have been redrawn (gerrymandering), the real fight has moved away from the middle and into the extremes. This is where each side tries to fire up its base during primaries instead of appealing to the center in general elections. Now, that same kind of tribal anger is spreading beyond politics and the internet and into college campuses, workplaces, and even family dinners at Thanksgiving.

Social-media platforms are not simply channels for communication; they actively amplify political anger and cause civic disengagement. For instance, one study found that exposure to political attacks on social media correlates with higher levels of cynicism and detachment from democratic institutions.[5] Meanwhile, research into the emotional effects of online networks shows that anger spreads more rapidly than positive emotion, making outrage both pervasive and contagious.[6]

Together, these dynamics contribute to a civic "doom loop." Stirred into frustration by what we see online, we conclude that our involvement won't matter. We pull back, and in turn are overlooked by politics and policymakers. We are not wrong in feeling insignificant; we are the effect of powerful algorithmic and emotional forces that shape online and political civic life.

Social media especially, but nearly all media, create echo chambers that are designed to expose us to fewer alternative ideas the more we spend time on these channels and platforms; what we're fed reinforces our preconceptions and biases. As one study into polarization concluded:

> The media exacerbates pessimism...Producers of local television's nightly news continue to follow the old media dictum that 'If it bleeds, it leads' by showing stories about

crimes and disasters first in their lineup every night. Cable news networks spend their entire day belittling the beliefs and behaviors of political candidates from across the political chasm they and their talk radio allies have helped to create.[7]

One intent of this book is to reverse this loop, to increase the visibility of ordinary people in politics, to get the negativity to stop, and to help those of us in the Exhausted Majority to get politicians to care more, listen more, and disconnect from big money more.

WE CAN STILL BE POWERFUL

Despite the powerful forces that would lull us into cynicism, rage, and disengagement, there is reason for hope. Across the country, when issues are put directly to the people, Americans rise above the noise. Time and again in recent elections, voters have broken through partisan gridlock and reminded us who we really are: a nation guided not by extremes but by the steady, common-sense convictions of a vast, moderate majority.

In several cases in state elections in 2018, 2020, 2024, and 2025, voters bypassed polarized legislatures to enact reforms with broad, bipartisan support, even in conservative states. For example, voters in Idaho, Nebraska, and Utah approved Medicaid expansion, in Michigan legalized recreational marijuana, and in Missouri approved medical marijuana. These ballot wins demonstrated a clear, cross-partisan readiness to solve problems that elected officials had been unwilling or unable to address.

In 2018, Florida voters passed Amendment 4 to restore voting rights to people with felony convictions, and states like Colorado, Michigan, and Utah approved redistricting reforms to curb gerrymandering.[8] Maine went further by adopting ranked choice voting for some offices, signaling a widespread appetite for this proven means of choosing fewer extreme candidates. When given the chance to vote directly on policy rather than through partisan representatives, voters—often including those in "Red" states—support pragmatic solutions that transcend party lines.[9]

Then, in 2020, the results in some states were striking because they happened during a presidential election year when polarizing rhetoric was at its peak. In this election, voters consistently chose pragmatic, cross-partisan solutions over ideological positions. This validates the Exhausted Majority research. In deep-red states like Missouri and Oklahoma, voters approved Medicaid expansion, ensuring health coverage for low-income residents, and in Florida, nearly 65 percent supported a higher minimum wage.

In 2024, voters in Washington, DC passed Initiative 83 which introduced ranked choice voting and opened primaries to independent (unaffiliated) voters. Initiatives in South Dakota and Ohio that would have made gerrymandering unlikely failed, however, revealing the difficulty reform efforts face, especially where the proposal is opposed by entrenched powers.

Abortion is a hotly contested issue but one where a large majority of the Exhausted Majority agrees. Since 2020, abortion ballot initiatives have shown how direct democracy can bypass deadlocked legislatures and give voice to the political middle.

By 2024, after the *Dobbs* decision, a surge of ballot measures let citizens decide directly. In seven states—Arizona, Colorado,

Maryland, Missouri, Montana, Nevada, and New York—voters approved constitutional amendments protecting abortion rights. (Nebraska was the one state where restrictions advanced: While a pro-rights measure failed, a rival amendment to limit abortion after the first trimester passed.)

Now, 2025. Maine voters approved Question 2, a statewide initiative establishing "extreme risk protection orders" (often referred to as "red-flag" laws) allowing courts to temporarily restrict firearms access for persons deemed dangerous. This passed by 63 percent to 37 percent, again showing the preference of most Americans for moderation.[10]

Also in 2025, Californians voted on Proposition 50, which passed with about 64 percent in favor to 36 percent opposed. Under this measure, the legislature would temporarily take over congressional redistricting (for the 2026–2030 election cycles), replacing the independent citizen's commission. The maps produced under this change are projected to enable the gain of up to five U.S. House seats for the Democratic Party.

These results reveal how moderate majorities can move beyond legislative stalemates when given the chance and often show a decided preference for initiatives that are fair and balanced and that protect democracy.

STEPPING INTO YOUR POWER

One way, perhaps the easiest, to move into your power, is to counter the perception that "We're all polarized." When we let this claim slide without comment, it reinforces our disconnection from one another and empowers those who profit from this perception: news organizations, social media, and many politicians.

What might you say if you hear someone lament, "There's so much polarization in our country"?

How about this: "We feel polarized because the loudest voices in politics tell us we are. But I'm aware of research that says otherwise." Or you might simply say, "This is a myth. Most of us are not extreme."

If you are a peace-loving individual who generally sees the best in others and wants a world in which we live and let live, you are in the *majority* in America. Your job—our job—as members of this group, is to find one another, stop listening to newscasters, politicians, and pundits who tell us we hate one another, and work together to start demanding that our politicians get this country back on track. The Exhausted Majority has the numbers and clout required to force change. If enough of us step into our collective power and remember that democracy bends toward justice when ordinary people exert their power, we can put our country on a better path.

In this chapter, we have named the Exhausted Majority and reclaimed the truth: We are not powerless extremists but a quiet super-majority yearning for common purpose. In the next chapter, we look at what broke our politics and how, in turn, it's breaking our sense of belonging, connection, and trust.

KEY IDEAS IN THIS CHAPTER:

* America feels polarized because our *political class and media ecosystem* are polarized; the public, largely, is not polarized.

* The Exhausted Majority wants problem-solving and compromise, not culture-wars or purity tests.
* Structural features such as gerrymandering, closed primaries, big money, and outrage media mute moderate voters and reward extremes.
* Direct democracy in the form of ballot initiatives often reveals the center's will: When voters decide policy directly, pragmatic solutions usually win.
* Power returns to the people when moderates re-engage together: voting, organizing locally, and insisting on structures (e.g., ranked choice voting, fair districting maps) that reward coalition building.

2

> We are the heirs of a great national idea—that human dignity is equal for all, and that the freedom to think and speak and worship as we choose is the birthright of every American.
>
> —JOHN MCCAIN, FORMER REPUBLICAN SENATOR

> We may feel stressed, overwhelmed, numbed, and afraid. But beneath these feelings, we still desire learning, freedom, and love.
>
> —MARGARET WHEATLEY, WRITER, SPEAKER, AND ACTIVIST

Broken Hearts and Broken Politics

How Declining Social Capital Weakens Democracy, Enables Extremism, and Creates a Spiritual Crisis

This chapter wasn't easy to write, and it may not be easy to read. But if I'm going to tell the whole *We the People* story, I must speak plainly. The story in this chapter is not all bad news, but it describes a country with deep problems that demand our involvement. In this chapter, I explain two of those problems: civic decline and spiritual despair.

If you can't bear another word about what's wrong, skim or skip ahead. But know this: *We the People* will never climb out of the hole we're in if we pretend it isn't there.

And what hole is that? It's the one we've dug by drifting away from being neighbors, from being people who stay connected with one another and join together to fulfill the promise of our communities and our country. Into that vacuum, dark forces have moved: cynicism, suspicion, loneliness, and a creeping sense of purposelessness. These aren't just private struggles; because this is so widespread, they are symptoms of a nation that has forgotten how to act in concert.

It wasn't always this way. This chapter tells America's story in two earlier frames—the 1830s and the era from 1890 to 1965—then contrasts those times with today. I begin by talking about the lives of earlier Americans not because they were perfect—they weren't—but because they regularly engaged in the practices democracy requires, habits that are far less common today.

Please be clear: By describing America's past in favorable terms, I am not pining for a return to yesteryear or saying we need to "Make America Great Again" (MAGA). Instead, I'm saying that, for the sake of liberty, we need to learn lessons from our past and apply them to our present and future. We aren't going back to the 1830s or any other point, nor should we. Our task is to put back in place democracy-enabling features of community life. Only *We the People* can do this.

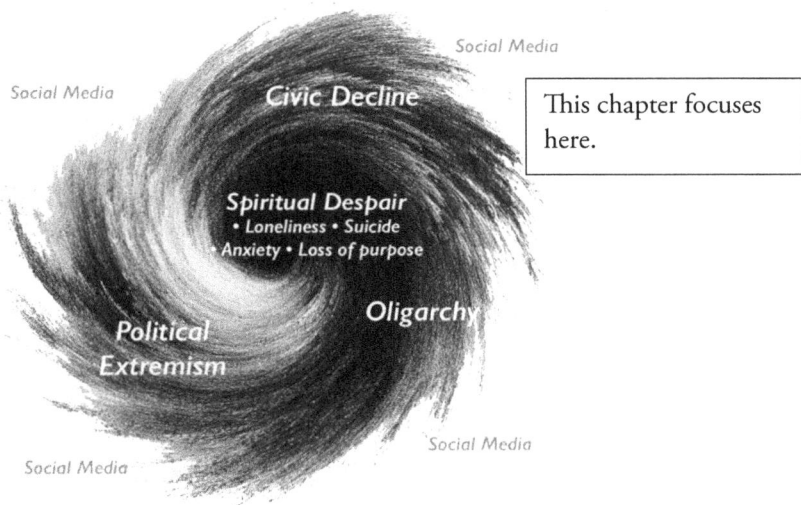

Social Media

Civic Decline

Social Media

Spiritual Despair
• Loneliness • Suicide
• Anxiety • Loss of purpose

Political Extremism

Oligarchy

Social Media

Social Media

Social Media

This chapter focuses here.

This chapter describes the risks to democracy created by Civic Decline and the Spiritual Despair that comes with this and the other two forces.

AMERICA IN THE 1830S

I begin with the America that a young French aristocrat and political thinker, Alexis de Tocqueville, encountered in 1831, just fifty-five years after the nation's founding. He crossed the Atlantic not simply out of curiosity but on a mission for the French government, which was grappling with the turbulence of its own political transitions in the decades following the Revolution. France had cycled through monarchy, republic, empire, and another monarchy, and its leaders wanted to understand how a democratic society might actually function.

Tocqueville traveled across the United States asking questions that felt urgent for his own country: How does democracy work in practice? What supports must be in place to sustain it? And what must citizens do to make it flourish? He captured his observations in *Democracy in America.*

Tocqueville answered these questions by conducting dozens of interviews over nine months with everyone from local officials to farmers. He sat in on town meetings and studied voluntary civic associations. He pored over public records, court documents, and newspapers, seeking to understand how ordinary citizens learned to be self-governing. It seems hard to believe now, but no one knew the answer to this; American's themselves were figuring it out.

Today, we take democracy for granted, but Tocqueville didn't. The United States was the first enduring democracy the world had known since ancient Athens.

Imagine traveling with Tocqueville in 1831, crossing a young America by steamboat, by stagecoach along rutted roads, and on horseback. The air smells of wood smoke and river water. Your boots are always muddy. In one town after another, you see him listening and inquiring, at taverns, courthouses, and in church halls as farmers, merchants, and ministers debate their common affairs. You can see him after the meeting chasing down the farmer who couldn't get permission to flood his field: How did the farmer feel? Would he withhold taxes? Would he drop out of civic life?

Tocqueville concluded that American democracy thrived through a rare and self-reinforcing combination of forces: local self-government, where citizens learned the habits of participation, a vibrant network of voluntary associations, where they practiced cooperation and compromise, and shared religious values, which, even when diverse in form, provided the moral compass and sense of duty that drove democracy.

He discovered that Americans were really good at a few things: formulating an argument, making that argument in a public forum, submitting it to a vote, and then *often losing*. Then, Americans would get over it and move on. If hard feelings arose, Americans, Tocqueville found, smoothed them over.

Tocqueville found that democracy only works when citizens actually show up and participate in civic life, while holding a kind of civic faith grounded in what might be called enlightened self-interest. In this, he uncovered democracy's superpower, a widely held belief, that one's own welfare was intimately connected to the common good: If I support my community's wellbeing, *my own* well-being is enhanced. Americans, he found, looked after their own interests by looking out for the interests of the neighborhood and the community. In short, Americans saw themselves as joined in common cause.

In contrast to what Tocqueville observed, in today's America, civic engagement has declined significantly. We just don't engage with others the way we once did. The Survey Center on American Life, for example, found that "relatively few Americans report participating in local meetings, attending community events, or volunteering regularly. Fewer than half (44 percent) of Americans say they attend a social event in their community...Even fewer Americans say they volunteer (28 percent) in their community at least a few times a year."

This is pronounced when we look at the young: 33 percent of young adults aged 18–24, in a 2024 survey, indicated no intention to participate civically, and an equal number said they are not currently engaged in community activities of *any* kind.[11]

Tocqueville observed that Americans learned democracy by practicing it: participating in town meetings, serving on juries, joining voluntary associations. Americans then obtained civic knowledge through daily participation in democratic life. As populations shifted to big cities, we supplemented civic participation with civics education in schools. But even this has been fading away.

In defense of present-day Americans, when Tocqueville studied our country, it was a nation of about 13 million people living mostly in small towns with simple institutions. Further, political leaders then were on a first-name basis with most of their constituents and a religion-driven moral framework encouraged good works and civic involvement. Today's America of 330+ million people entails vast cities, huge bureaucracies, global corporations, digital networks, and complex lives. Direct civic participation, for most, is far more difficult. In addition, today's Americans live with declining religious participation, increased geographic sorting by ideology and social class, and social media echo chambers that reinforce division.

Economic inequality has also grown steadily in modern times, further eroding civic life. Tocqueville observed an America that was far more homogeneous economically than ours is, meaning that there weren't the vast gulfs between income classes that we have today. In Chapter Three, we will learn how the wealth gaps of today's America undermine our felt sense that we're all in this together, a perception Tocqueville considered essential for democracy.

We may never return to the America Tocqueville described, but we can still become the nation the Founders envisioned: imperfect yet striving, capable of self-correction, and working largely in concert with one another. That future is possible if we're willing to learn from the past and apply its lessons to our own time.

AMERICA—1890–1965

As we move ahead in our history and see America modernize, we learn that America's civic story is an undulating rhythm of gain and loss. America's history is that of a nation building its civic strength, then losing it, then building it again. Yet within those rises and falls lies a hopeful truth: We have rebuilt before, and *We the People* can do it again.

To understand our civic story, we need to examine the period that represents both democracy's greatest challenge and its greatest comeback. It begins with the period from 1890 to 1910, known as the Gilded Age. The years around 1890 represent one of the lowest points in American social cohesion. Democracy was listing then, too, yet Americans found ways to right the ship.

This was the period in which fiercely competitive industrial titans like Andrew Carnegie, Jay Gould, and John D. Rockefeller amassed enormous fortunes by harnessing new technologies (steam, rail, electricity, telegraph, assembly lines), exploiting cheap labor, bending government policy to serve private power, and crushing competitors, all the while accumulating unprecedented wealth. These men created exploitative labor conditions and built an economy in which the top 1 percent controlled around 40 percent of national wealth. They gained the moniker "robber barons" because of their exploitative methods.

As this was occurring, farms mechanized, displacing workers. Industrial jobs in big cities beckoned, but for most

Americans migrating to the big city jobs, it was a broken dream: Farmers and small-town folk found employment in the cities, but along with this came dangerous working conditions, twelve-hour workdays, and starvation wages.

The farm-to-city migration caused decline in social cohesion. As people left the countryside, they also left behind tight-knit communities where most people knew each other, the kind of community ties Tocqueville had observed sixty years earlier. In cities, these workers found themselves isolated in tenement buildings, working alongside strangers, cut off from extended family networks and community institutions that had provided support and meaning.

Researchers use the term "social capital" to refer to what these Americans were losing. Sociologist Robert Putnam, in his book, *Bowling Alone,* defines this as "connections among individuals and social networks, and the norms of reciprocity and trustworthiness that arise from them." In simpler language, it is the value we get when we are connected to supportive social groups, and within those groups, our relationships are characterized by trust and cooperation. In short, when we have social capital, we help one another and build trust. All of this is essential for democracy to function.

The story of the Gilded Age era is remarkable for what happened once working conditions were at their worst: Putnam's social capital curve, pictured below, started going higher and higher. It did so until around the mid-1960s, with only a dip for the Great Depression and through two World Wars.

The social capital curve rose steadily in part because grassroots reform movements began to spring up and press for change. The agitation generated by them was amplified by countless sermons condemning sweatshop labor and by best-selling exposés from the era's "muckrakers." All this brought deplorable working conditions and widespread exploitation into public view. In response, unions emerged, laws were passed to curb unsafe practices, and child labor regulations took hold.

Social Capital Since 1890

Upward Slope:

- Union membership grows
- Service organizations born (Kiwanis, Lions)
- Church membership high

Kennedy Administration Televisions now in all homes.

Social Capital is the value we get when our relationships with one another are characterized by trust and cooperation.

Downward Slope:

- Union membership declines
- Service organizations decline
- Church membership declines

1880 1890 1900 1910 1920 1930 1940 1950 1960 1970 1980 1990 2000 2010 2020 2030

During this same period, the women's suffrage movement gained momentum, and organizations like the Young Men's Christian Association (YMCA) and Young Women's Christian Association (YWCA) created new civic networks that drew people into shared purpose. Together, these forces helped knit communities more tightly and generated the kind of social capital that allowed democracy to deepen.

Then came World War I, accelerating the growth of social capital further through military service, war bond drives, and victory gardens. Home-front mobilization created shared national experiences and, after the war, organizational networks sprang up that persisted long after.

When the 1930s brought the Great Depression, the Roosevelt administration responded by creating massive civic infrastructure that further built social capital: New Deal programs drove the construction of community centers, libraries, and civic buildings while employing millions and creating places for people to gather. Social Security, passed during this time, gave Americans strong confidence in the federal government, another form of social capital.

World War II (WWII) accelerated social capital acquisition yet again. Most Americans experienced a strong sense of shared purpose even though serious race-based exclusions and injustices persisted. In the war, young men from the south served alongside northerners, farm kids served with city-dwellers, building trust across social boundaries. The home front mobilized entire communities through rationing boards, civil defense, war production, and volunteer efforts. The GI Bill sent millions of (white) veterans to college and provided loans for returning (white) veterans. Then, after the war, veterans' organizations flourished, adding again to social capital.

After WWII, suburbanization, powered by affordable cars, new highways, and the housing boom, helped generate new civic forms: Parent-Teacher Associations (PTAs), Little League teams, neighborhood associations, and countless local clubs. Union membership and attendance at places of worship reached historic highs. The post-war economy produced the strongest middle class the world had ever seen.

Income inequality fell to record lows; by the 1950s, the top 1 percent held only about 10 percent of national wealth, down from roughly 40 percent in 1900. Rising wages, broad access to education, and expanding homeownership (far more available to whites than Black Americans) fueled mobility and confidence. Trust in government was high, and despite ongoing civil rights inequities, social cohesion surged. Americans, as Robert Putnam famously noted, were joiners.

THE DECLINE OF SOCIAL CAPITAL, 1965 TO TODAY

Then, the rise of social capital stalled. The remarkable period of civic engagement and social cohesion that began in the 1890s began to sputter in the mid-1960s.

One cause was growing wealth inequality. From the late 1940s through the mid-1970s, productivity and wages climbed together: As workers became more productive, their pay rose. But beginning in the 1970s, the connection broke. For example, between 1979 and 2019, net productivity rose around 60 percent, while the typical worker's compensation rose by only about 16 percent.[12]

When workers see the economy growing but their own pay stagnating, it breeds distrust in business, government, and political leaders. Falling institutional trust is one of the clearest markers of declining social capital. Today, many Americans think the system favors the well-connected, and they're correct as we'll see in the next chapter. That perception powerfully shapes trust and participation. When some prosper while others fall behind—even when it only *seems* this way—envy, resentment, and status anxiety grow. That undermines the very essence of social capital, the sense of "we're all in this together."

The ethics and creeds of service organizations like Rotary, Lions, Kiwanis, and others tell a powerful story about social capital. These clubs emerged during the great civic upswing from 1890 to 1965, each with a creed members recited at every meeting. Rotary's famous *Four-Way Test* asked: *Is it the truth? Is it fair to all concerned? Will it build goodwill and better friendships? Will it be beneficial to all concerned?*

Imagine the culture-shaping force of millions of Americans repeating those questions weekly, holding themselves to a standard of truth, fairness, and the common good.

Membership in these clubs has been shrinking for decades; the average age of members is now nearing 70. As these organizations fade, we lose one of our most reliable on-ramps to belonging. When we lose places that once taught us how to show up, work together, and act in service to something larger than ourselves, we lose democracy's keystone.

Addressing this decline, in the days after the murder of conservative activist Charlie Kirk, Gov. Spencer Cox of Utah, the state in which Kirk was killed, was asked what he thinks gives rise to political violence. Cox, noting that the shooter appeared to be a lonely, disconnected person, said to the reporter that he often asks his audiences:

> How many of you belong to the Rotary Club? Or the Lions Club, an Elks Lodge—whatever volunteer organization? And maybe 50 years ago, almost every hand would have gone up. Now, almost no hands go up...Do you go to church on Sunday? Do you have people in your life outside of the virtual world where you can have dinner and have conversations and get to know each other better? (*New York Times*)

Political scientist Lilliana Mason, who studies polarization in America, has identified the critical importance of "cross-cutting" relationships in toning down strife and bitter feelings. By this term, she refers to associations that put one in contact with others whose backgrounds, outlooks, social class, and religion differ from one's own. Without these means of interacting with one another, society becomes more fragmented and social capital diminishes. America's service organizations serve as intermediary institutions between individuals and the state as do churches, but both are declining. In both settings, an attorney rubs elbows with the plumber, and both with a shopkeeper.

Perhaps the context in which the most elbow-rubbing used to occur was church, but since 1965, church attendance in the United States has fallen dramatically. This marks one of the most significant social shifts of the past half century. In the mid-1960s, roughly two-thirds of Americans attended religious services regularly; today, that figure has dropped to around one-third. This decline is especially steep among younger generations, many of whom describe themselves as "nones"— religiously unaffiliated. (Data suggests some decline among Jews, as well. According to a 2020 survey, only ≈20 percent of U.S. Jews—≈2.7 percent of Americans—go to synagogue at least once a month, down from ≈25 percent in a 2013 survey.[13] But attendance zamong American Muslims—about 1.1 percent of the population—has increased. According to a 2020 survey of U.S. mosques (the Institute for Social Policy and Understanding— ISPU), weekly Friday [Jum'ah] prayer attendance increased 16 percent from 2010 to 2020.[14])

The waning of organized religion has had profound social consequences. For much of the twentieth century, houses of worship were central hubs of American social life. Churches and other places of worship were and are places where people not only pray together but also build friendships, volunteer together, serve on committees, and learn the habits of cooperation. Membership in a church, synagogue, or mosque led and leads to membership in one or more of the many groups spawned by the church: Bible study, aid groups, softball teams. The decline of these institutions has left many Americans less connected to one another, weakening the civic bonds that once sustained communities and democratic life.

For generations, places of worship (mostly churches; Christians make up over 60 percent of Americans today) gave people not only a shared story and moral framework but also a place to be known, to feel needed, seen, and woven into the lives of others. As those institutions fade, many are left searching for substitutes and coming up short. Rates of loneliness have climbed, anxiety and depression are widespread, and a growing number of people report feeling unmoored or unsure of their larger purpose. This is not simply a matter of private spirituality; it is also a civic challenge. When fewer of us have places that call us into relationship and responsibility, our social fabric frays, and the work of sustaining a democracy becomes immeasurably harder.

Robert Putnam concludes his book, *Bowling Alone*, by saying, "By virtually every conceivable measure, social capital has eroded steadily and sometimes dramatically over the past two generations." As powerful as they are as contributors to this, the erosion of service organizations and decreased church attendance are just two factors in the decline of social capital. Putnam offers other causes for its decline. The percentages are his estimates of the relative contributions each of these things makes to the erosion:

* Pressures of time and money and two-career families: ≈ 10 percent
* Suburbanization, commuting, and sprawl: ≈ 10 percent
* Electronic entertainment, especially TV: ≈ 25 percent
* Generational change—the WWII generation being replaced by one with different values regarding community involvement: ≈ 50 percent

Putnam made this observation before the digital revolution reshaped daily life. *Bowling Alone* appeared in 2000, on the cusp of profound change, before the platforms that now dominate our attention even existed. In the years since, Facebook (introduced in 2004), Twitter (2006), Instagram (2010), Snapchat (2011), and TikTok (2016) have emerged—tools that amuse and to some degree help us but often erode personal ties and push us into echo chambers. Add to this the iPhone (2007), Netflix streaming (2007), Zoom (2011), and most recently consumer AI (2022), and the result is a culture in which convenience and connectivity frequently come at the expense of social capital.

As if this weren't enough, compounding it all is the pace of change, which has become mind-boggling and there is no end in sight. It sounds quaint now, but listen to Alvin Toffler, author of the international bestseller, *Future Shock,* worrying about the rapid pace of change in 1970 just as social capital was beginning to drop: "Change is avalanching upon our heads," he wrote, "and most people are grotesquely unprepared to cope with it." He had no idea what was coming.

In the current moment, AI is the technology driving change most. The *Harvard Gazette* reports that almost 40 percent of U.S. adults aged 18–64 had used generative AI tools as of August 2024, noting that this is "faster than the public embrace of the internet (20 percent after two years) or the personal computer (20 percent after three years, the earliest researchers could measure)."[15]

Toffler defined "future shock" as "the dizzying disorientation brought about by the premature arrival of the future." If this was an accurate characterization of America fifty years ago, we'd have to say today that something worse than dizziness has become our pervasive condition: Algorithms increasingly shape what we see and think about, and AI transforms professions faster than institutions and individuals can adapt. The avalanche Toffler warned about has not only arrived; it has become the new terrain we must somehow learn to navigate. The next section makes clear that many of us are failing the test.

BROKEN HEARTS

The social fragmentation described in the preceding paragraphs has created what President Joe Biden's Surgeon General, Vivek Murthy, called a public health crisis. He said we are facing "an epidemic of loneliness and isolation." This is because half of all Americans now report experiencing loneliness regularly, while an alarming 61 percent of young adults aged 18–25—describe their loneliness as "serious." Murthy told us that one in four American adults say they have no close confidants, no one to share their struggles or support them when things are difficult.[16]

Other numbers continue to tell this story, including the fact that Americans spend 70 percent less time with friends compared to a generation ago. Then, only 10 percent of adults said they lacked deep friendships, yet today, the average American has fewer close friends than ever, with about half reporting three or fewer and 12 percent saying they have none at all.

To some degree, our loneliness is self-imposed, evidently: Today, we don't even invite people into our homes, as we once did. Data from the American Time Use Survey indicate that since the early 2000s, Americans have significantly reduced the time they spend socializing in person. Recent studies show declines of 30 percent or more in face-to-face social time, especially among younger adults.[17]

The psychological and physical toll of all this has reached alarming proportions. Suicide rates have climbed 37 percent since 1999, making suicide the leading cause of death among those aged 10–34. Studies show that loneliness increases suicide risk by 26 percent. Social isolation is particularly devastating for men, whose suicide rates are now over three times higher than women's.[18]

Surgeon General Murthy called the accelerating rates of suicide, isolation, and cynicism a public health problem. For me, it's better termed a spiritual crisis. What else do you call a widespread loss of meaning and purpose?

The cruel irony is that our withdrawal from each other makes us more vulnerable to the precise fears that drive us apart. As Americans isolate, we create a self-reinforcing downward spiral: Isolated and desperate people become susceptible to victim mentality, subscribe to conspiracy theories to explain their troubles, and leave themselves open to authoritarian appeals. Meanwhile, the problems we face—climate change, economic inequality, racial injustice, and the rest—require the kind of collective action that our current social arrangements make almost impossible.

THE LOSS OF "THIRD PLACES"

Sociologists call them third places—the informal gathering spots outside home and work where people naturally meet, talk, and form the small ties that hold a society together. Cafés, parks, libraries, barber shops, churches, and community centers have long served this role.

Today, many third places have thinned out or disappeared. Remote work has hollowed out the workplace as a social hub, and church attendance is in decline. No surprise, then, that TikTok and Instagram are filled with young people lamenting the "lack of third places." Urban planners now warn of a growing Third Place Crisis.

Yet new forms are emerging. Bookstores, board-game cafés, climbing gyms, and coworking lounges are booming precisely because they offer what people are craving: community, informality, and human presence. Public libraries are experiencing a renaissance with Gen Z. Even Starbucks built its early success by explicitly marketing itself as a third place. And the Mamdani campaign provided a temporary third place for its nearly 100,000 volunteers.

This matters for democracy. Third places are where trust grows, differences become familiar, and civic muscles quietly strengthen. Rebuilding them may be one of the most powerful ways to renew the bonds of citizenship.

THE DEMOCRATIC IMMUNE SYSTEM

To stay healthy, democracy, like the human body, depends on an immune system. Just as we rely on defenses to fight infection, a healthy republic rests on overlapping sources of resilience. When these defenses weaken, the whole system becomes vulnerable. This is exactly what we see today.

We've been exploring two of those defenses—social capital and mental health. Nonprofits, unions, churches, and neighborhood groups once gave Americans belonging and voice. As they weaken, so does democratic immunity. Economic security matters too. When wages stagnate and inequality grows, people lose faith that the system works for them. Pluralism, the idea that all groups are legitimate and have a stake, adds another safeguard, but it too is under pressure as we'll see in Chapter Four.

Some defenses do exist, of course. For example, at every level—neighborhood, municipality, even nationally—there are leaders with integrity and everywhere can be found citizens who share and act upon civic values. Others are less obvious and some are under threat, but they do exist and are just as critical: a free press, impartial courts, fair elections, and nonpartisan officials. These are antibodies that resist abuse of power.

Civic education is another shield, but this, too, is in decline. When citizens understand their history and institutions, they are harder to deceive and more likely to engage. Equally important are norms of restraint and fair play: compromise, truth-telling, respecting election outcomes. That erosion shows up whenever politics becomes more about winning the moment than preserving the structures that lets us differ.

And finally, the most basic layer is everyday civic habits. Small acts like helping a neighbor, volunteering, and showing up may seem trivial, but they build trust and bring people together. When these layers overlap, they make democracy resilient.

The same things that make a community a good place to live are the same things that enable democracy to thrive. A project called Weave: The Social Fabric Project has measured every community in the United States to see how it stacks up. The organization uses three metrics of trust to assess a community. You can find out how your own measures on each dimension by going to trust.weavers.org and entering your zip code. No wonder I love my own community: It gets high scores on all three trust indicators.

Trusting behaviors. This democracy enhancing measure has to do with how actively people engage in the community by joining clubs or committees, volunteering, donating to nonprofits and participating in local elections or school/public meetings.

Trusting intentions. This facet gets at the attitudes and intentions people hold toward one another and their community; whether people feel others are trustworthy, whether they follow local events and organizations, and whether they express support for initiatives to strengthen the community.

Trusting Spaces. Does the community have easily accessible physical or social spaces that facilitate connection? This might include libraries, barber shops, coffee houses, and parks where people meet, talk and build relationships.

America's civic nature is formed in many ways and in many places including town halls and soccer sidelines, mosques and megachurches, gun-safety groups and hunting clubs, PTAs and volunteer fire companies. Wherever people meet regularly to serve something bigger than themselves, social capital grows.

STEPPING INTO YOUR POWER

There it is—the hole we're in. Hard to read about, right? In this chapter, we traced the story of social capital from the high of Tocqueville's America, where civic faith and neighborly cooperation were everyday norms, through its great buildup from 1890 to 1965, to today's fractured landscape of sorting, isolation, inequality, and tribalism.

If we have any hope of addressing what's wrong, we must look squarely at the costs of civic decline and what it does to us. And importantly, as I've said before, all of these problems can be turned around—if *We the People* work together.

None of us want to think of our country as being so off-kilter. Our time is a heartbreaking dark valley in our national story. Our current story is a tale of personal unhappiness and the erosion of democracy's magic, the dense web of trust and shared experience.

But hear this: The present unraveling is not our destiny. If we see this as temporary, not a permanent condition, we are more powerful. As we summon our determination to turn things around, to become more connected to one another, to join with one another in common cause again, we can right our ship.

The path upward begins the same way it always has: when ordinary people decide to act. As we acknowledge and speak more boldly about the sadness we feel at the loss of community, of what democracy means to us, as we join others to rebuild its foundations, we begin the climb back.

You might name the feeling differently. Maybe it's not sadness for you but frustration, maybe even fury. Anger is real, and it's justified. But anger almost always sits on top of something more vulnerable and tender: a sense of loss, disappointment, or fear that what we value is slipping away. Recognizing that deeper layer doesn't make us weak; it helps us be clearer about what's at stake. When we can name what hurts, we're better able to decide what to do next and to act with purpose rather than just react.

Putnam's social capital curve rose for seventy-five years before it fell. The people who lifted it weren't heroes but ordinary citizens who took action by marching for labor rights, suffrage, civil rights, and environmental protection. The decline that began in the 1960s isn't fate; it's the sum of choices about how we spend time, whom we trust, how we connect, and what kind of society we tolerate. We can make other choices.

The fact that you've read this far perhaps suggests that something is already stirring in you, as it is in so many Americans, a recognition that something vital is missing from our common life. Maybe you also feel, as millions of your fellow Americans do, a longing to recover what that missing element is. That spark is where renewal begins. We can't go back to the 1830s or the 1960s, nor should we. But we can turn to face the present bearing fresh resolve, rebuilding the democracy-enabling features of community for our own time. In doing so, we restore not just our civic health but our mental and spiritual health as well.

If democracy falters when social trust collapses, as we've been exploring here, it crumbles when concentrated wealth tilts the field. That, too, we must face, and we do so in the next chapter. What you've read in this chapter and the story ahead may seem dark, but knowledge is the first step toward power. When we understand what ails us, we begin the work of repair.

KEY IDEAS IN THIS CHAPTER

* Democracy works when neighbors build neighborhoods and communities together; it falters when we isolate.
* From the Gilded Age to the post war boom, civic networks built resilience; since the mid-1960s, those bonds have diminished.
* Declining trust + rising isolation → a vulnerable republic; rebuilding social capital is democratic self-defense.
* The kind of renewal we need won't come from nostalgia or from Washington; it starts locally in our social habits, the places we build and spend time in, and through organizations that reconnect us.
* The descent we see isn't destiny: Millions of small, consistent acts can bend the curve back toward belonging and shared purpose.

3

We may have democracy, or we may have wealth concentrated in the hands of a few, but we cannot have both.

—LOUIS BRANDEIS

The tyranny of a prince in an oligarchy is not as dangerous as the apathy of a citizen in a democracy.

—MONTESQUIEU, ENLIGHTENMENT PHILOSOPHER

Of the Rich, By the Rich, For the Rich

The Perils for Democracy of Putting So Much Wealth Into the Hands of the Few

When prosperity is shared, when markets serve people rather than the other way around, democracy works for everyone. But when wealth and power concentrate in a few hands, as it does today, when large numbers of people experience their economic lives as precarious, and when success seems reserved for the powerful and well-connected, people's faith in the system begins to erode and democracy's institutions falter.

There is good reason to believe this is where we are. In this chapter, I will use the word "oligarchy" to refer to the economic system that is emerging in our country. Oligarchy is an economic system that concentrates wealth and power in the hands of a small elite who control capital, major corporations, technology, and media, and as a result, have outsized political influence.

The story of modern America is not only one of disordered politics, civic decline, and widespread mental health problems, but also one of political capture: Oligarchic wealth funds campaigns and think tanks and controls media ecosystems and lobbying enterprises that protect its privileges, all while driving up distrust across political and class lines. When ordinary Americans see that political influence follows money, they lose faith that their voices matter, and then, they disengage. When the rewards of the economy flow to a tiny elite, people begin to suspect that the whole game is rigged and populist demagogues rush in to exploit that resentment. This is well underway.

Modern oligarchy began in the late 1970s, as the rules of the American economy began to be rewritten. Deregulation began in earnest, unions were stymied, tax cuts for the wealthy began to proliferate (they haven't stopped), and shareholder-first capitalism took hold. Government was defined as a problem under Reagan, markets as the solution. Citizens began to be turned into consumers. What had once been an economy that balanced—or at least did a better job of balancing—the interests of business with the noncommercial interests of the public shifted into one that valued efficiency and profit above all else.

Under Ronald Reagan's influence—he was president from 1981 to 1989—policymakers and corporate leaders embraced a new creed: Government is the problem and markets are the solution. Deregulation spread from airlines to banks, taxes on the wealthy were slashed, unions were weakened, and corporations were told their only duty was to maximize shareholder value.

Also, during this era, a shift occurred in how business leaders saw their role. For instance, CEOs who once spoke about stewardship and responsibility began speaking instead about efficiency, competitiveness, and the imperative to put shareholders first.

As a result, factories began to close, jobs went overseas, and the financial sector swelled. At the same time, a subtle but profound cultural change took hold: Americans were redefined less as citizens bound by shared responsibility and more as consumers defined by personal choice.

In the decades since, the value of accumulating wealth has been sold to us as freedom. If everyone pursues their own gain, this argument goes, we will all be better off. But the result has been precisely the opposite: As a very small number of Americans has progressively cornered the wealth of our nation, the results are stagnant wages, skyrocketing inequality, fragile communities, and a hollowing out of the civic institutions that bind people together. The promise that capitalism and democracy would rise together has given way to a new reality: The wealthiest Americans have multiplied their fortunes, while most others have been asked to work harder and longer for less.

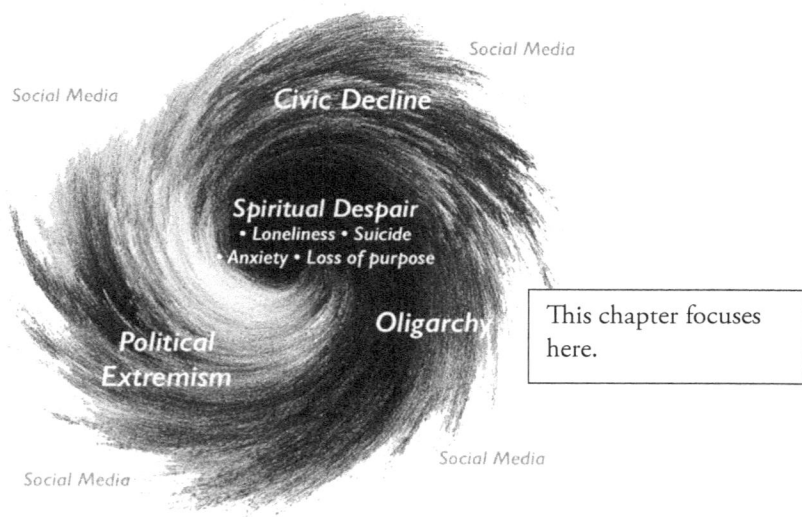

Social Media
Social Media
Civic Decline
Spiritual Despair
• Loneliness • Suicide
• Anxiety • Loss of purpose
Oligarchy
Political
Extremism
Social Media
Social Media

This chapter focuses here.

NUMBERS

As I write in 2025, we often hear how well the economy is doing, but prosperity is not broadly shared. Those apparently good economic numbers are a façade built on credit cards, debt, and anxiety.

Data tells the story starkly. I begin with a statistic that, to me, is breathtaking and sad: Despite our supposedly good economy, fully 60 percent of Americans live paycheck-to-paycheck. This means that most Americans are one pay period away from not covering rent, food, or medical bills; they live without a margin or safety net. One unexpected car repair, illness, or expense of two or three hundred dollars can trigger a personal crisis for a huge number of Americans.

Along with this, American households now carry a staggering amount of debt: over $18 trillion in total as of mid-2025, with nonmortgage consumer debt alone (credit cards, auto loans, student loans) running in the trillions.[19] According to USAFacts and Federal Reserve data, the average U.S. adult carried roughly $63,000 in total debt in mid-2025. Excluding mortgages, that figure drops to about $20,000 in consumer debt per household—mostly from credit cards, auto loans, and student loans. On this debt, on a national scale, U.S. households pay roughly $120 billion per year in credit-card interest and fees alone.[20]

This burden of debt helps explain why the economic lives of so many Americans are so precarious. When a large share of one's income must go to paying credit card and other debt, there is little or no margin left for unexpected expenses. According to the financial institution Lending Tree, as of the second quarter of 2025, Americans owed about $1.21 trillion in credit-card balances. Consumer Financial Protection Bureau data shows that, on this debt, card holders are paying an average of ≈ 22.8 percent.

As credit lines become lifelines, household budgets become brittle. Consumer debt both reflects and deepens economic insecurity. It is a structural symptom of a market society that expects individuals to borrow their way through instability rather than rely on stable wages, buffering social systems like food pantries, or public support. When surviving economically takes all one's energy, there's little left for community life, volunteerism, or political participation.

People living this close to the edge, people who understandably feel the system is rigged against them, are not only vulnerable but also often angry and distrustful of a system that seems unfair, making them susceptible to populist appeals, fueling political extremism and weakening patience with and trust in democratic processes and institutions.

Who benefits when ordinary Americans have so much debt? The top 1 percent of Americans has captured nearly all income growth since 1980. At the same time, since 1979, even though productivity has risen by 65 percent, typical wages have grown only 17 percent. Meanwhile, over that time, CEO pay has sky-rocketed by more than 1,200 percent, outpacing both inflation and productivity by a staggering margin. Today, CEOs make more than 340 times what the average worker earns.[21]

Astonishingly, in the United States, a mere dozen indi-viduals now hold more wealth than entire nations do. Those 12 people collectively possess more money than the bottom half of all American households combined—roughly 165 million people. Think about that.

With fortunes this large, superrich individuals can shape policy, fund or block political movements, influence tax laws, and control major media or tech platforms. In effect, they can act as *unelected co-governors* of the republic. When a handful of individuals can spend billions to steer elections or policy debates, the very idea of representative government gets called into question.[22]

Our era compares to some degree with the Gilded Age in terms of wealth concentration. In 1910, the top 1 percent of earners owned 45 percent of the wealth. Today, the small group composed of Musk, Zuckerberg, Larry Ellison, Bezos, and a few others own approximately 30 percent of the wealth. Then, as now, a laissez-faire ethos prevailed; corporate lobbying, favorable tax laws, and campaign-finance laws allowed then and continue to allow today vast influence by the wealthy. The names have changed, but the story hasn't. The same golden hand still writes the rules and threatens democracy.[23]

While ordinary workers have made zero progress economically, the billionaire class has flourished. The RAND Corporation estimates that roughly $79 trillion has shifted over the period 1975–2023 from the bottom 90 percent of Americans to the top 1 percent. This breathtaking transfer of wealth is one of the largest in human history. This is not just inequality. This is extraction on a breathtaking scale.[24]

OLIGARCHY KILLS (INNOVATION)

Today, few Republicans speak out about the perils of putting so much wealth into the hands of the few, but in earlier times, many Republicans did so, including Abraham Lincoln, Reconstruction leaders, and Teddy Roosevelt. Those voices associated wealth concentration with slavery, economic monopoly, and threats to democracy.

Teddy Roosevelt, for example, spoke vehemently against the dangers of concentrated wealth and oligarchic power, describing these as mortal threats to democracy and fair competition. In his 1910 *New Nationalism* speech, he warned that "special business interests too often control and corrupt the men and methods of government for their own profit," urging Americans to "drive the special interests out of politics." He later declared, "Behind the ostensible government sits enthroned an invisible government owing no allegiance and acknowledging no responsibility to the people." Were he alive today, he would scarcely believe that we did not heed the lessons of the past.

By definition, oligarchy concentrates power in the hands of a tiny minority. Those oligarchies depend on stability and hierarchy. It turns out that these inhibit innovation. Innovation thrives on curiosity, experimentation, and the willingness to overturn the status quo. That tension explains why oligarchic systems may generate short-term prosperity in proscribed sectors and for a few while innovation generally sputters.

One dramatic example of this comes from our own history. The pre–Civil War South was a plantation oligarchy built on slave labor. In that system, the wealthiest 1 percent owned nearly all the capital as well as the means of production (slave labor). The incentive of the planters was to defend the existing order and suppress change. Because they did so, they invested little in education, infrastructure, or technological development beyond what directly increased the productivity of slavery. Meanwhile, the North industrialized, built railways, and fostered a culture of engineering and experimentation, as the South remained economically narrow and technologically stagnant.

The long-term effect was catastrophic for the South. When war came, the Confederacy faced an enemy with vastly superior manufacturing capacity, rail networks, and inventive energy. These are precisely the advantages that enable more open, pluralistic economies to prosper. The South lost the war because, by its end, it could not get its soldiers to the front (not enough rails), could not provide them with weapons (not enough steel mills), and could not clothe them (not enough textile mills).

Another example of how oligarchy impedes progress is the USSR of yesteryear and the Russia of today. After the collapse of the USSR, vast state industries were privatized at breakneck speed. A handful of men—oligarchs—acquired enormous wealth and influence, effectively fusing political and economic power. In theory, Russia was transitioning to a market democracy; in practice, it became a petro-state oligarchy. The country's wealth concentrated in energy and natural-resource extraction, forms of fixed capital analogous to the South's dependence on land and slaves. The long-term result is today's Russia, a society dependent on imports, one that is chronically uncompetitive, technologically backward, and locked into an authoritarianism that protects the wealth of the oligarchs.

Make no mistake: The United States today is far better off than Russia. But wealth and power are again concentrating in a narrow elite. A handful of technology and financial firms shape not only markets, but also, in the case of social media, discourse (worsening it) and, disturbingly, imagination itself. Platforms owned and controlled by the tech oligarchy decide which voices are amplified and which are buried, what we see and what we don't. These platforms govern attention—the new currency of power—through algorithms that are far better at rewarding outrage and conformity than fresh thinking and open-mindedness. Like the cotton barons of the nineteenth century and the Russian energy oligarchs of today, the incentives of America's current oligarchs lean toward preservation, not renewal; their empires depend on control, not creativity, on constriction, not freedom.

Against this stands the American experiment, a system dependent on a broad middle class empowered to build, imagine, and take risks. America flourishes when opportunity is diffused, when invention and ownership are shared. Oligarchy impedes all of this. Without an empowered middle class, democracy begins to drift toward a new kind of plantation, gleaming, digital, and perhaps efficient, but ruled by a few.

OLIGARCHY KILLS (PEOPLE AND DEMOCRACY)

As wealth and power concentrate at the top, social spending, worker protections, and shared goods like education, healthcare, and cultural institutions all face pressure and begin to wither. The result is predictable: Poorer families and disadvantaged regions face worsening health, housing, and nutrition, while stress and instability spread through the population.

Consider this: Since 2010, U.S. life expectancy has stagnated or declined, even as billionaire wealth has quadrupled over that time frame. And this is occurring in the richest country in the history of the world. This is unseen in other wealthy democracies. Today in the United States, life expectancy for the richest 1 percent of men is fifteen years longer than for the poorest 1 percent.[25]

To this sobering story needs to be added the most recent statistics about so-called "deaths of despair," a term popularized by economists Anne Case and Angus Deaton to describe deaths from suicide, drug and alcohol poisonings, and chronic liver disease. From 1999 to 2021, among Americans aged 25–74, the rate of these combined causes rose approximately 2.5-fold, making deaths of despair the fifth-leading cause of death by 2021.[26]

From 1999 to 2017, the age-adjusted death rate from these causes rose from roughly 22.7 per 100,000 to about 45.8 per 100,000—an increase of more than 100 percent. Within that total, drug overdose deaths alone have quadrupled, driving much of the overall surge. In the words of the Joint Economic Committee, "Mortality from deaths of despair far surpasses anything seen in America since the dawn of the 20th century."[27]

The market ethos driven by the relentless drive to accumulate wealth has seeped deeply into our social fabric. The logic of the marketplace is maximize your advantage, minimize your costs. This mentality inevitably begins to pervade how we think about and treat one another. As Martin Luther King Jr. warned, when the means *by* which we live—money, markets, and material success—outdistance the ends *for* which we live, democracy itself begins to lose its soul.

This market-driven worldview adds to the loneliness so widely experienced in our country today. When we live our lives on screens and platforms, people retreat into isolation. The rise of social media, engineered for attention and profit, mirrors the broader economy: To tech barons, users are not citizens in conversation but data points to be monetized. And, if profit demands, what users are delivered should outrage them: Algorithms amplify outrage because outrage sells. In a society where greed is rewarded, even our emotions become commodities.

THE MORAL LOGIC OF WEALTH

For moral and civic renewal, we need a politics and an economy that speak on behalf of fairness, the common good, for community and patriotism in a new way.

My reading of the research into how the rich see things, however, tells me we can't depend on the wealthy to lead the way. It turns out that possessing wealth tends to create its own moral logic. We know from psychological research that the more wealth you have, the more you see the world as fair. Wealthy individuals tend to see their own advantages as the result of their hard work (and many do work hard), not because the system is unfair and they enjoy privileges that most Americans don't have. Though there are exceptions, research makes clear that most rich people do not acknowledge the advantages they have received from inheritance, education, or networks as crucial in their success. (By contrast, some philanthropists like Abigail Disney, Nick Hanauer, and Morris Pearl have spoken publicly about "born-on-third-base" privilege.)[28,29]

Other research reveals that wealth tends to close one off from awareness of the suffering of others, creating what some researchers call an "empathy gap." As one consequence, the wealthy underestimate how much the average family struggles. Surveys show high earners guess median U.S. income is about twice what it actually is. In turn, this misunderstanding fuels opposition to minimum wage hikes, rent control, unionization, and other initiatives that help ordinary Americans get ahead.[30]

Every economic order rests on a story of who deserves what. The story America tells its wealthiest citizens today is that their wealth reflects their virtue and is visible proof of their hard work, talent, and courage. Those who have studied this phenomenon in depth tell us this is not malice so much as a coping mechanism: a way of reconciling vast inequality and privilege with a belief in justice.

If the wealthy comfort themselves with a distorted story of personal merit, those who live paycheck-to-paycheck carry its shadow. The 60 percent of Americans who live paycheck-to-paycheck have been told the same story that the rich have been told: Success is earned, hard work brings reward. But these Americans do not have success. In trying to achieve it, they have been willing to work double shifts if necessary, juggle costly childcare, pay their bills late, and maintain the faith that if only they work harder, things will work out. Yet progressively, the horizon of stability has moved farther away from them. For fifty years, wages have stagnated, rents have risen, and the cost of healthcare, education, and housing have gone higher and higher. Most Americans are no better off. But wealthy people are.

When wealth is moralized to mean that only the good deserve it, struggling to make ends meet becomes shameful, and people begin to internalize failure. Struggling people begin to think, *If I'm struggling, it must be my fault.* Self-blame is corrosive. It makes collective will almost impossible to muster and replaces solidarity with widespread feelings of futility and unworthiness.

Surveys show that most low- and middle-income Americans still admire the self-made rich; they want success, not resentment. But beneath the surface lies a steady erosion of belief in fairness, in mobility, in the promise that the system rewards effort. When that belief falters, civic trust falters with it.[31]

What grows in its place is ambivalence toward wealth and the wealthy. While nonwealthy Americans admire those who seem to have made it, they resent the arrogance and distance of elites. They see billionaires dominate politics, media, and technology, they watch them live and travel in luxury, while their own lives are squeezed daily by forces they can't even name or understand. They feel invisible to the people who make the rules—and are. And because it's painful to believe the system is rigged, many become open to the influence of politicians who claim to be interested in saving them. Sadly, those would-be saviors are some of the very people rigging the system.

Arguably, democracy can survive inequality—it has been doing this off and on for our entire history—but cannot survive the conviction by a majority of Americans that the game itself is rigged. When the rules no longer seem fair, people stop playing the game, or worse, they cheer for anyone who promises to break it.

MADISON'S WARNING

James Madison, one of America's Founders and our fourth president, wrote: "Justice is the end of government. It is the end of civil society. It ever has been and ever will be pursued until it be obtained, or until liberty be lost in the pursuit."

Here, Madison uses the word *end* to mean *purpose*. Government exists, he argued, to secure the common good and protect the rights of all. When those rights are not safeguarded, justice erodes; and when justice erodes, liberty follows. In Madison's view, government is the instrument by which competing interests are balanced so that no faction can dominate the rest.

By my reading, we are no longer in balance.

Madison warned that when the pursuit of justice gives way to the pursuit of power, liberty goes away. Oligarchy ensures the loss of liberty because in this type of system, a small group claims the benefits of government for itself using law, policy, and influence, not to secure justice but to preserve its own advantage.

Partly due to Madison's influence, the American Founders designed checks and balances to guard against this danger. Yet when wealth and influence concentrate in too few hands, those safeguards weaken. The machinery of democracy continues to turn, but the pursuit of justice, its core purpose, goes out of focus. What remains is not self-government but rule by the powerful under the pretense of liberty.

HOW GENEROUS ARE AMERICAN BILLIONAIRES?

America's 900 billionaires (Investopedia) are often praised as magnanimous, civic-minded benefactors, and some are, but the numbers paint a different picture of the class as a whole. Data shows that most give a tiny fraction of their wealth, often controlling how contributions are spent, thus minimizing impact.

Much of the wealth intended for charitable works is parked in foundations and donor-advised funds which offer tax advantages and control over distribution while delaying or limiting beneficial impact. Critics call this system "philanthrocapitalism"—a form of giving that mirrors the inequities it claims to solve.

U.S. billionaire wealth surged by roughly 88% from 2020 to 2024. (Institute for Policy Studies) (Think about that for a moment.) In contrast, charitable contributions by this group over that period rose only about 6.3%. This is hardly a compelling display of largesse or social stewardship.

Elon Musk, the richest person in the world, is remarkably ungenerous, so much so that his foundation, which holds over $14B in assets, has come to the attention of the Internal Revenue Service (IRS) because it has failed to give the minimum of 5% of its investments each year for the past several years. (*New York Times*)

A generous person of means asks, "How can I use my wealth to make the world better?" rather than "How can I use it to preserve my status and privilege?" yet this is what is occurring in most cases. Exceptions include individuals like MacKenzie Scott—Jeff Bezos' ex-wife—and Laurene Powell Jobs—Steve Jobs' widow—who take a much more generous approach, giving large sums quickly, directly, and with few restrictions.

ECONOMY AND DEMOCRACY

Oligarchy is ugly, and the threat it presents to democracy is both real and vivid. But greed is not the inevitable ethos of any society, and it certainly isn't for our country. The rules that create the conditions that foster oligarchy are made by our elected representatives and can be changed. The same ingenuity that designed the shareholder economy could, if guided by different values, design an economy that better serves the common good.

There is a moral question beneath the study of any economy, an ancient one: *What is the economy for?* We have come to accept that the answer in our country is maximizing profit, growth, consumption, and shareholder return. But the moral foundation of democracy calls for a different answer. The economy in the American story must exist to sustain the conditions a free people require, institutions that enable families, neighborhoods, and communities to flourish.

Even Adam Smith, the eighteenth century Scottish moral philosopher whose work laid the foundation for modern economics, writing the year the Declaration of Independence was signed, said that a "commercial society" is just one part of the human condition. For him, the moral character of the people is the *ultimate measure* of their humanity. Smith believed markets must be embedded in a society of trust, fairness, and sympathy. If that is so, then our economy must enable dignified work, community flourishing, and shared agency, not reduce ordinary people to the status of disposable inputs or consumption units.

Democracy works and can only be sustained when citizens work in dignified circumstances, earn a living wage, and can share equitably in the rewards of productivity. When ordinary Americans who aren't billionaires are treated as disposable inputs to someone else's quarterly earnings, democracy is more than an illusion; it's a lie.

Our capitalistic system needs reform, but this task is not about rejecting a market-based system; it is about redefining what markets are for. Markets are tools, not the purpose; *democracy* is the purpose, human flourishing is the purpose.

Across the country, experiments are already emerging: employee-owned companies that distribute wealth fairly; community land trusts that keep housing affordable; public banks that invest locally; and cooperative models that give workers a real voice in decision-making. These are not utopian dreams but pragmatic acts of reconstruction by people of goodwill trying to restore the link between economic participation and civic belonging.

Many young people are resonating with Bernie Sanders's rallying cry against oligarchy. In 2025, he and Alexandria

Ocasio-Cortez (AOC) brought their *Fight Oligarchy* tour to many so-called "red" states and districts, drawing, for example, some 34,000 people to Denver's Civic Center Park, 20,000 in Salt Lake City, and huge crowds in many other Republican-majority cities. These large crowds are a reminder that anger at concentrated wealth and power transcends party lines.[32] (See the Appendix: What the Exhausted Majority Really Believes, for data on this point.)

Young people heard more than an economic message from Sanders and AOC; they heard a civic and moral one. When Sanders says that concentrated wealth produces concentrated power, and concentrated power is the death of self-government, young people listen. This is not a new message. As Justice Louis Brandeis warned a century ago, "We can have democracy in this country, or we can have great wealth concentrated in the hands of a few, but we can't have both."

STEPPING INTO YOUR POWER

The economic forces we've been exploring in this chapter are big. Each of us is small. It's very difficult to know what to do about any of this. We tell ourselves that we're powerless. That feeling is real, but it's also the result of living inside a system designed to make ordinary people doubt their own agency. When everything seems optimized for someone else's benefit, it's easy to assume there's no meaningful role for us to play. But history suggests otherwise.

It's understandable to feel small when the system seems tilted toward those with money, access, and influence. But disengagement is exactly what this system counts on. Every time you resist the pull toward cynicism, every time you speak about an issue that matters to you, every time you vote—especially in a low-turnout local election—you reclaim a bit of ground. Your power begins with refusing to believe that you don't have any.

Democracy was not created with capitalism in mind. The Founders imagined a republic of citizens, not consumers, an economy of small farmers, merchants, and craftsmen bound by civic duty, not global markets. This is a far cry from capitalism in its modern industrial and financial form.

At its best, capitalism can amplify freedom and reward innovation; at its worst, it concentrates power and hollows out the very equality on which democracy depends. The Founders feared tyranny in any form, whether by kings, mobs, or greedy business owners. Capitalism can coexist with democracy *only* when democracy has the courage to discipline it.

Democracy is not just a form of government but a moral bond, a shared promise that we rise or fall together. Most Americans still understand instinctively that freedom cannot survive without fairness. To face our democratic crisis honestly, we must reckon not only with political extremism, civic decline, and loneliness but also with the economic system that amplifies them all. Restoring democracy will take more than ensuring fair elections; it will require rewriting the economic rules so that decency and contribution are rewarded more than greed. Only *We the People* can compel that shift.

If these things matter to you, stay with it. No one is asking you to fix them alone. But if you take your feelings seriously— your frustration, your sadness, your hope—you will find your way into the company of others who are working to set things right. Chapter Eight, "Effecting and Sustaining Change," has references to national organizations that are working to redress economic inequities. Read about them, consider joining their efforts.

The next chapter explores how a narrow, ideologically driven minority has gained power far beyond its size and what that reveals about our political and spiritual condition. Thus, our dark story deepens. Yet the truth is the health of our democracy has always rested with the many, not the few. If even a fraction of the Exhausted Majority stands up for fairness and decency, renewal is not only possible but also inevitable.

KEY IDEAS IN THIS CHAPTER

* Democracy depends on shared prosperity. When wealth and power concentrate, trust and participation collapse.
* Since the 1970s, economic rules have increasingly favored the rich. Deregulation, union decline, and shareholder capitalism shifted power upward.
* Concentrated power kills innovation and hope. Oligarchies defend privilege, not progress—from the pre–Civil War South to modern Russia.
* Inequality erodes health and life itself. "Deaths of despair" have more than doubled since 1999 as life expectancy for the poor falls.
* Market logic has invaded civic life, turning citizens into consumers and communities into marketplaces.

4

When fascism comes to America,
it will be wrapped in the flag and
carrying a cross.

—SINCLAIR LEWIS

I've never thought of the United
States as a Christian nation. I think
we ought to be one of faith where
people can choose their faith freely.

—GEORGE W. BUSH

Tyranny of the Minority

*How a Determined Minority Has Put
Our Democracy at Risk*

Many times in this book, I have taken pains to say that most
Americans are not filled with hatred for others but instead
want to find peaceable ways to resolve our problems and move
forward together. I've said that most of us are not extreme and
are comfortable with the reality that in a democracy we aren't
always going to get our way.

I have also said that there are some who aren't willing to expose their ideas to the public marketplace, people for whom the phrase *We the People* means "Only us." These people are the subject of this chapter.

This is a minority of about 20–30 percent of Americans who have a set of demands about who Americans are and should be, what religion we should have, and who should be able to decide how things go. They think they are the "real Americans" and should decide for the rest of us what is best for our country. In this chapter, I will describe that group and the misguided views it has with respect to our democracy. I will show that, in truth, they don't want democracy at all.

But before I do this, I have a happier task. I will explore with you a concept that is crucial to fully understanding who we really are as a country.

PLURALISM

As I've tried to understand what ails our country and also what is extraordinary about it, I've rediscovered a beautiful and wondrous idea that is indispensable to what America means and stands for. It can be stated in one word: pluralism.

Pluralism seems like a complicated legal term, but it's not. At its root, it simply means a belief in the multitude, in the many. Think of the Latin phrase on the dollar bill: *E Pluribus Unum.* This phrase means "out of many, one." When we speak of pluralism in the context of government, we refer to a system where multiple groups influence policy- and lawmaking, not just one group. It turns out that this is America's unique guard against the authoritarian rule of a king, what transforms us from subjects into citizens, a topic covered in depth in Chapter Five.

The Founders were very clear that in a democracy, power should be distributed far and wide. Doing this, they reasoned, would be the antidote to tyranny. In a system like this, each citizen and each group of citizens holds power. This was unheard of historically, but the Founders felt this would be the only way democracy, a system of self-government, could work.

Pluralism means shaping a government where all voices, not just the loudest, the richest, or most powerful, have a say and where the rights of those in the minority are protected. It begins with the recognition that people will always see the world differently. The Founders didn't see diversity as a flaw to fix but as the lifeblood of democracy itself. They believed that disagreement, handled with respect, could make us stronger, that out of many voices, a common good could and would emerge.

To ensure that the populace would choose compromise over conflict, the Founders put in place government structures to create the formal and informal channels necessary for different groups to voice their concerns, compete for influence, and negotiate solutions. These would include everything from public hearings, legislative committees, district courts, and Constitutional protections.

When the Founders said in the First Amendment to the U.S. Constitution, *"Congress shall make no law respecting an establishment of religion, or prohibiting the free exercise thereof,"* they were enshrining pluralism. As we will learn later, some very powerful political actors in our country are trying to eliminate pluralism and protections for pluralism, including the separation of church and state.

Pluralism assures freedom but is also decidedly practical. Social psychological and group dynamics research has long established the value to innovation of varied viewpoints. When differing perspectives are brought to bear on an issue, the result is more creativity, better problem-solving, and far greater group cohesion. Societies that squelch pluralism, as we saw in the last chapter, usually stagnate, culturally and economically.

Finally, pluralism in our system of government embodies the ethical idea that all people have dignity and worth. The Founders revered this idea because they knew that *rejecting* pluralism opens the door to persecution and authoritarianism. When only one group's ideas are valued, coercive demands of conformity are sure to follow.

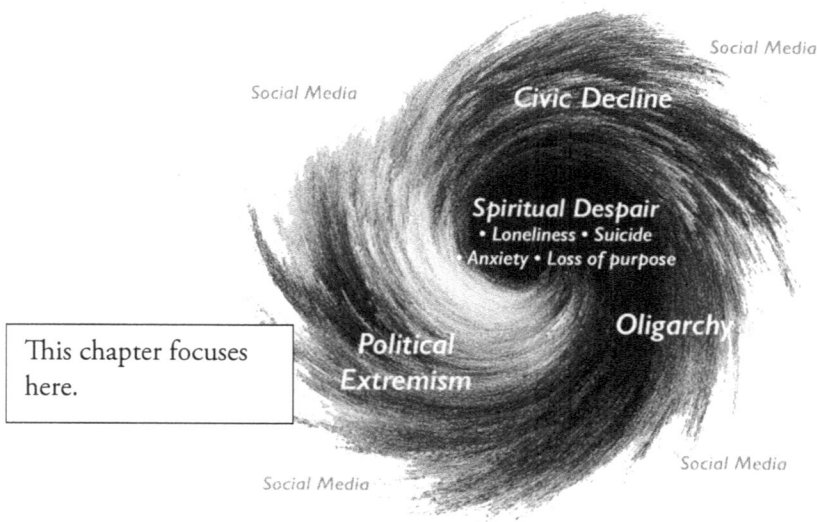

Social Media

Social Media

Civic Decline

Spiritual Despair
• Loneliness • Suicide
• Anxiety • Loss of purpose

Oligarchy

This chapter focuses here.

Political Extremism

Social Media

Social Media

NATIONALISM: THE ENEMY OF PLURALISM

Contrasted with pluralism is nationalism. Nationalism is a political perspective emphasizing the centrality to citizenship of national identity, family history, shared religious tradition, strong borders, and usually male dominance. These things, nationalism's adherents believe, are the foundations of a healthy America.

We need to explore this idea because we're at a point in our history where a minority devoted to nationalism has gained considerable power and is attempting to move our country away from the value of pluralism. If it succeeds, we lose our democracy.

Those who promote nationalism abhor what they see as their political and cultural enemy: Liberal progressivism. This term means a system of individual rights, equality, social reform, and, yes, pluralism, all aimed at justice and inclusion. Members of the nationalist movement hold that if liberal progressivism prevails, western civilization ends. This is why they want to end it. This may sound outlandish, like a wild conspiracy theory, but it is not. Have you ever heard of Steve Bannon? He is very open about this. Does the name Tucker Carlson ring a bell? He does, too. So did Charlie Kirk. Trump is more guarded in his statements, but he wants this as well.

It may surprise you to learn that, currently, the loudest and most powerful voice for nationalism in the United States is J.D. Vance, who has spoken far and wide in support of nationalism.

A speech by Vance on July 5, 2025, at the Claremont Institute is illustrative. This organization, through its publications and affiliates, actively promoted and disseminated false narratives and conspiracy theories questioning the legitimacy of the 2020 election. In this speech, Vance repeatedly returned to themes of heritage, gratitude, sovereignty, and skepticism of mass immigration, all but saying that our country is one in which people like him—native-born, white, and Christian—are the only true Americans. In that speech, Vance said the far left is threatening what Americans like him hold sacred, claiming that liberals repudiate the vision he laid out. He described liberals as infatuated with pluralism and putting far too much stock in the Founders ideals.[33] (The speech can be watched on YouTube.)

In these remarks (and many places elsewhere before and since), Vance articulates the view that animates much of the extreme right: Being an American is about your history and your forebears' history more than anything you believe in, e.g., the ideals of democracy or civil rights. In the Claremont speech, Vance suggested that Americans whose ancestors fought on the Confederate side in the Civil War have more claim to citizenship than any naturalized citizen does today, or, for that matter, any progressive does.

In this speech, Vance articulated one of two stories that have always embroiled our country in opposition. One is rooted in the ideals of the Founders of our country. The other is the story articulated by and fought for by the planters of the American South. It turns out that the Civil War still rages.

The first story—the Founders' story—is the familiar one rooted in "all men are created equal," "life, liberty, and the pursuit of happiness," and, crucially, pluralism. It holds that all people possess a natural right to freedom and to pursue happiness as they see fit. It recognizes that we differ in background, language, worship, and heritage and that each difference contributes to the American fabric. This story rests on a covenant: a promise to live together in peace despite our disagreements. Lincoln at Gettysburg and Martin Luther King Jr. on the Washington Mall carried this story forward.

The opposing story, born in the slaveholding South and revived today by parts of the far-right, claims that an American is a white landowner, uniquely entitled to liberty because others are less deserving. Its ideal nation resembles ancient Athens or Rome, where a privileged few enjoyed freedom and the rest were meant to serve.

With modest updates, this is the story J.D. Vance and his allies advance, namely, a nation defined by whiteness, Christianity, and nativism, where diversity is a threat, equality is conditional, and freedom belongs to the few, while obedience is expected of the rest.

To be clear, most Americans don't buy what Vance and the Claremont Institute are selling. In but one study, conducted by Salve Regina University's Pell Center for International Relations and Public Policy, 63 percent of Americans chose the civic ideal of equal rights and freedom over a nationalist story of shared heritage and loyalty.[34] Many other studies confirm that same finding.

J.D. Vance and others on the far-right disparage pluralism for what they believe it has produced: most vocally, the growing visibility of transgender people but also what they describe as uncontrolled immigration, confusion about gender roles, undue emphasis on women's rights, and a redefinition of marriage they reject. They rarely use explicitly racist language, but the story they promote unmistakably centers and protects whiteness. And the policies they favor would sharply restrict religious, cultural, and social pluralism—the very diversity that has long been one of America's greatest sources of strength.

What pluralism looks like © 2025, Richard McKnight

When I use the term "the far-right," I'm referring to a constellation of overlapping factions: MAGA populists, National Conservatives, and Christian nationalists, along with affiliated think tanks, media networks, and activist groups. These range from formal institutions such as the aforementioned Claremont Institute and America First organizations to online movements and militias that fuse nationalism, religion, and claims of being "true Americans."

Yoram Hazony, a founder of the National Conservative movement with which Vance identifies and author of *The Virtue of Nationalism*, contends that America's Founders made a colossal mistake in elevating pluralism as a guiding ideal.

To Hazony and his followers, pluralism erodes strength and leads to cultural decay. They argue that a nation built on competing moral and cultural frameworks cannot sustain coherence or loyalty. They maintain that liberal tolerance erodes the shared faith, hierarchy, and traditions that once anchored American society. In their view, the modern celebration of diversity—religious, ethnic, ideological—has dissolved the moral consensus necessary for order. What they offer instead is a restoration of "the Christian nation" they claim the Founders intended.

While Hazony, Vance, and others claim the Founders were "misguided" in enshrining pluralism, James Madison's writings stand as a repudiation. Pluralism, Madison argued, was designed into our system because both liberty and stability demand it. Madison's solution to the potential threats of tyranny and instability wasn't to suppress differences but to multiply them. "Extend the sphere," Madison said, "and you take in a greater variety of parties and interests; you make it less probable that a majority of the whole will have a common motive to invade the rights of other citizens."

Madison argued that the greatest threat to liberty came not from a solitary tyrant, but from internal factions that might oppress minorities. Today, however, due to the phenomenal success of the extreme right-wing in winning elections, the danger is inverted: A determined minority, having seized the machinery of power, now seeks to oppress—and *is* oppressing—the majority.

Watching the right-wing coalition from the other side of the political spectrum, many on the left think those on the right have lost their moorings. Don't they want what the Founders wanted, they ask? The very disturbing answer is no; they don't. What they want is to fundamentally change the nature of our country.

CHRISTIAN NATIONALISM

Those on the far-right believe that the Founders' pursuit of equality and progress has led to cultural and spiritual decline, not liberation. They tell us that the basis of our country is the Christian religion and that liberal democracy and Communism alike erode and are hostile to traditional culture. The founding documents of America, prominent authors in this movement believe, contain pernicious seeds.

One example is *The Benedict Option: A Strategy for Christians in a Post-Christian Nation* by Rod Dreher (2017), who argues that Western liberalism has become spiritually corrosive, undermining faith, family, and moral order. He urges Christians to withdraw from mainstream institutions and build intentional communities to preserve "orthodox" faith and culture. The book treats liberal democracy as an unsustainable experiment that must give way to a more explicitly Christian social order.

Another is *The Case for Christian Nationalism* by Stephen Wolfe (2022), in which the author contends that nations are divinely ordained along ethnic and religious lines, that governments should explicitly privilege Christianity, and that liberal equality and pluralism are inherently destructive to moral life. He argues that America should abandon Enlightenment ideals in favor of a "Christian commonwealth." Faith communities, across traditions, have long been engines of service and belonging. They hardly ever attempt to fuse their theology with state power. This stands in contrast to Christian nationalism.

Some leaders in the Christian-nationalist movement have begun speaking as though saving the nation and saving the faith were the same task. As just one example, in promoting his book *Under Siege,* Eric Trump said in an interview, "We're saving Christianity. We're saving God. We're saving the family unit. We're saving this nation." To use a phrase, Heaven help us.

This remark captured the goal revealed by Christian-nationalist rhetoric: the fusion of divine and political missions. But it also revealed the tension inside the movement. Eric Trump's words were too much even for some Trump supporters. David Closson, director of the Family Research Council's Center for Biblical Worldview, pushed back: "Eric Trump's comments, I think, fail to appreciate that Christianity predates the Trump administration." He added that Christianity does not need saving.

The vision behind Christian nationalism, more than any other factor, is what has enabled this minority to gain power. This highly organized and well-endowed minority seeks to set up Christianity as a state religion. And its adherents have convinced themselves that God is on their side. Meanwhile, the Exhausted Majority stands flatfooted, barely understanding who this group is and what it is trying to achieve.

While most Americans want pluralism, especially religious pluralism, the Christian nationalism movement does not. Broader attitudes toward diversity confirm the trend: A Pew Research Center survey found that 64 percent of U.S. adults believe that an increasing number of people from different races, ethnic groups, and nationalities make the country better.[35] According to the Becket Fund's 2022 Religious Freedom

Index, Americans' support for religious pluralism reached a new high, with the "Religious Pluralism" dimension scoring 84 out of 100.[36]

Contrast this with the views of Christian nationalism. Researchers at PRRI (Public Religion Research Institute) define a Christian nationalist as a person who agrees ("Sympathizers") or strongly agrees ("Adherents") with five propositions. Note how agreement or strong agreement with each puts one in tension with the value of religious pluralism[37]:

* God has called Christians to exercise dominion over all areas of American society.
* The U.S. government should declare America a Christian nation.
* Being Christian is an important part of being truly American.
* If the United States moves away from our Christian foundations, we will not have a country anymore.
* U.S. laws should be based on Christian values.

According to PRRI, 29 percent of Americans agree or strongly agree with *all five statements*. As one writer wryly remarked, "In other words, adherents and sympathizers of Christian nationalism comprise about 30 percent of the U.S. population. But somehow, they manage to make up two-thirds of the Supreme Court."[38]

By state, North Dakota and Mississippi lead with 50 percent of the population supporting these views. Several states are over 45 percent: Alabama, West Virginia, Louisiana, Arkansas, and Oklahoma.

Add all this up and you see a false vision of America that, Amanda Tyler, leader of Christians Against Christian Nationalism (CACN), summarizes this way:

> The United States was founded as a Christian nation, based on Christian principles, and has a special role to play in God's plan for humankind. If our leadership or national values stray from traditional Christianity, God will withdraw his blessings from the nation.

As Tyler points out, Christian nationalists would have you believe that what unites the people of our country is Christianity. But nothing could be farther from the truth. What unites us is the right to believe whatever we wish or to have no belief at all. What unites us—and what the Founders assured us we would have—is the right to be who we are.[39]

Christian nationalism conflicts with pluralism and, if any of those five propositions were to be enacted, our democracy would suffer a fatal blow.

I would be remiss if I did not also note the malignant intentions of this faction with respect to race. The objections to DEI—diversity, equity, and inclusion—that we hear so much about under Trump, are clearly racist, disdain pluralism itself, and fly in the face of the perceptions of a majority of Americans about the state of race relations.

To the latter point, standing against claims by the Trump administration that racial bias and discrimination are things of the past, a 2023 survey by Pew Research Center found that 64 percent of adults say the legacy of slavery still affects Black Americans "a great deal" or "a fair amount," and 57 percent say the United States has not done enough to give Black people equal rights.[40] A Gallup study in 2024 found that 73 percent of Americans say race relations are "bad," and 58 percent say they are getting worse.[41] In each of these studies, there are marked differences across party affiliation with Republicans agreeing at lower rates than Democrats. Studies by PRRI and AP-NORC validate these findings.

The opposition of the right-wing to DEI programs isn't merely tactical or policy-based; their objections are deeply rooted in racial anxiety and animosity. The hostility of this group toward DEI initiatives reveals the anxiety of some whites about America's changing demographics and their own racial status in our changing world. As is well known, the majority status of whites—and most on the far right *are* white—is projected to disappear by the 2040s.

When Trump and his minions attack DEI programs, characterize immigrants as invaders, erase the historical record of the contributions of Blacks and other minorities, impose on cultural institutions a whites-preferred view of history, and restore Confederate statues, they are challenging the very idea that America should be a place where people of different backgrounds, identities, and experiences can participate fully in civic life. One has to ask what kind of democracy we are if the color of our skin determines how we're treated by the system meant to protect us?

WHY CHRISTIAN NATIONALISM IS GAINING GROUND

This menace to democracy is gaining ground for at least three reasons: Christian nationalists vote at very high levels, they are as organized as any movement ever has been, and they are deeply funded. Adding an impetus that cannot be under estimated, many movement leaders frame politics in spiritual warfare terms, which mobilizes supporters ("God is on our side, not theirs").

In the words of Katherine Stewart, long-time observer of the movement and author of *Money, Lies and God: Inside the Movement to Destroy American Democracy*:

> American democracy is failing because it is under direct attack, and the attack is not coming equally from both sides. The movement described in this book isn't looking for a seat at the noisy table of American democracy; it wants to burn down the house.

Stewart, who has studied this movement for over twenty years, explains in the documentary *God And Country* that Christian nationalists have disproportionate influence in our politics...

> ...precisely because they have [an] infrastructure that serves to turn out the vote in disproportionate numbers. In a country where 40-50 percent of people don't vote, you don't need a majority to dominate an election cycle. All you need is a disproportionately activated and motivated *organized minority*. [my italics]

Evidence of how well the movement is organized can be seen in Project 2025, the blueprint guiding the Trump administration. This long and detailed plan includes language about "biblical principles"; critics warn this would move the United States away from strict church–state separation. Russell Vought, the architect of this document and avowed Christian nationalist, is now a top Trump administration official.

I'm writing this in the days after the murder of Charlie Kirk. In the *Atlantic*, writer Stephanie McCrummen said something that illustrates how deep the tentacles of this movement have become embedded in our government. She wrote,

> At Kirk's memorial service..., Defense Secretary Pete Hegseth described the moment at hand as 'not a political war' and 'not even a cultural war'—it's a 'spiritual war.' Followers believe that a fresh outpouring of the Holy Spirit is under way...for them, spiritual warfare is a matter of combatting demonic forces and bringing all of government and society under God's dominion.[42]

Charlie Kirk pushed tirelessly for the "Seven Mountains Mandate," the idea that Christians are called to dominate seven spheres of society, from government to education to business. In Kirk's teaching, reclaiming cultural and political dominance in these arenas is not merely a political project but a divine decree, an obligation to God to reassert Christian authority over institutions that, he argues, have been captured by secular and progressive forces.

As mentioned earlier, many in this movement openly advocate eliminating the separation of church and state. One, Mike Johnson, Speaker of the House, has said, "The Founders wanted to protect the church from an encroaching state, not the other way around." This is far from the truth. Justice Clarence

Thomas has argued the Establishment Clause may not apply at the state level.

Christian nationalists are fiercely resolute in their intentions and increasingly flirt with violence to get their way. Nearly four in ten Christian nationalism sympathizers (38 percent) and half of Christian nationalism adherents (50 percent) agree that "because things have gotten so far off track in this country, we need a leader who is willing to break some rules if that's what it takes to set things right."[43]

Some statements by prominent figures, including J.D. Vance, have been interpreted by critics as normalizing political coercion. Recent polls by Ipsos, Pew, and others reveal that, depending on how the question is framed, 25 percent–40 percent of Americans think violence might be necessary, too, but most of those identify as Republicans. Any hint of legitimizing violence should be rejected out of hand. This is not how Americans deal with their differences.[44]

I've been presenting Christian nationalism as a political menace, and this is certainly true. But it is also treacherous morally and spiritually. Daily, in Trump's public statements, we see repeated examples of falsehoods and inflammatory rhetoric that create moral injuries. As we learn of his plan to use the military to enforce domestic laws, send immigrants to prisons in countries other than their own, and force cultural institutions to rewrite their accounts of American history, I find myself wondering: Where is the compassionate Jesus in this?

Russell Moore, editor-in-chief of *Christianity Today*, ordained Baptist minister, and outspoken critic of Christian nationalism (and personal hero), criticizes Christian nationalism for treating

Christianity as a cultural or political identity rather than a transformative faith rooted in the gospel. He calls Christian nationalism "idolatry," maintaining that it is "an extrinsic religion," one that "enables people to claim Christianity without following Christ" and "to convince themselves that they are goose-stepping to heaven."[45]

Trump and many of the people in his movement are not merely morally flawed and theologically confused individuals but they also position themselves as warriors in a political, cultural, and religious army that normalizes, even admires, the use of malice, dishonesty, cruelty, and authoritarianism to get what it wants. This is not just a political dispute we all must stand against. We must also see it as the moral outrage it is.

HOW CHRISTIAN NATIONALISTS GAINED POWER

If you want to learn more about Christian nationalism and how its adherents have gained power in politics, the best book to read is Katherine Stewart's *MONEY, LIES, AND GOD: Inside the Movement to Destroy American Democracy.* For now, I'd like to highlight one important way this movement has expanded their reach in politics by examining a powerful organization called the FFC.

This organization was founded by Ralph Reed in 2009. Reed, a very influential political architect, mobilizer, and strategist in the religious right system, launched FFC with the explicit goal of positioning evangelical and conservative Catholic voters as a permanent political force within the Republican Party.

These activities help answer the question, "How can a minority of voters win so much influence?" The Faith & Freedom

Coalition is well funded and laser-focused. It pours tens of millions of dollars into elections and backs a policy agenda centered on abortion restrictions, "religious liberty," opposition to LGBTQ+ rights, and strong support for Israel.

FFC's real power lies in turnout. Through state chapters and church networks, it runs highly organized get-out-the-vote operations aimed at evangelical and conservative Christian voters in swing states. Using sophisticated voter databases, it scores households by likelihood to vote, targets them with mail, calls, and in-person visits, and floods churches with millions of voter guides.

The results have been visible. Between 2016 and 2024, Trump's share of Hispanic and Black voters rose sharply— enough in key states like Georgia, Arizona, Nevada, and Pennsylvania to help him build a winning coalition.

Remember Tony, the highly mobilized Christian nationalist, and Ashley, the anxious disengaged moderate? They embody the imbalance we've just traced: a fervent minority versus a

FAITH & FREEDOM COALITION   HOME ABOUT ˅ ISSUES ˅ NEWS CONTACT 🅕 ❌ 🅞 🅞   DON

EMPOWERING VOTERS: FAITH & FREEDOM'S GRASS ROOTS ELECTION DAY EFFORTS:

$63 MILLION	**32 MILLION**	**10 MILLION**	**130,000**	**10,000**
dedicated to 2024 voter registration, education, and turnout	evangelicals and Catholics engaged	doors to be canvassed	churches engaged	grassroots volunteers activated

From the Faith and Freedom Coalition Website

checked-out majority. If this minority continues to consolidate power, we face a dark future—Christian-nationalist dominance and prolonged constitutional breakdown. But there is also a third path: democratic resilience. I explore these scenarios in Chapter Eight.

STEPPING INTO YOUR POWER

In *Separation of Church and Hate*, John Fugelsang offers a line that stops you cold in its moral clarity: "The overwhelming majority of progressive, moderate, and even conservative Christians, Jews, and Muslims," he writes, "are getting along just fine...just trying to make their way through life and leave a better world for their kids."

He is right. Religion is not the problem. The danger comes when faith is weaponized, when extremists twist what should be sources of humility, service, and love into tools of domination and control. Across traditions, fundamentalism warps the moral core of religion. When Christian nationalists, or any zealots, fuse rigid theology with political power, the result is not compassion but coercion. The threat is not belief; it is the demand that everyone else submit to it.

Understanding how a committed minority can bend institutions may feel unsettling, but it can also be clarifying. Small groups shape outcomes all the time. The question is which groups we choose to join. You don't need to mobilize the entire country; you need only to stand with those who share your values, many of whom are already doing the work and would welcome you in.

Extremists remain a minority. Most people of faith live quietly and generously alongside those who believe differently, all the while feeding the hungry, comforting the grieving, strengthening their communities. This decency is simply drowned out by the noise of those who crave power more than Christian love and self-righteousness more than the mercy demanded by their savior.

Recognizing danger is only the beginning. Democracy asks us to answer it, with agency, not with despair or fury. The next chapter turns toward that work: the inner habits and outward practices that help us move from spectators to stewards of our republic.

KEY IDEAS IN THIS CHAPTER

* Pluralism = freedom in practice. It protects dignity, disperses power, and provides a way to turn disagreement into problem-solving.
* Nationalism is pluralism's rival; it elevates one identity and creed over others, inviting coercion and authoritarianism. Nationalism demands conformity and worships power; patriotism calls us to love the nation enough to make it better.
* A motivated minority—Christian nationalism—can dominate when the majority is disengaged. Organization beats ambivalence every time.
* The stakes are moral as well as political: Censorship, anti-DEI backlash, and "spiritual warfare" rhetoric diminish who counts as a "real" American.

＊ Renewal is still possible: If the Exhausted Majority reengages—votes in larger numbers, supports reforms (fair districting maps, open and ranked choice voting primaries), and rebuilds cross-community ties—these moderates can bend the future toward democratic resilience.

PART II
Recovering Our Power

Having faced what's broken, this section asks *Who must we become to repair what's broken?* Here, we recall and reclaim one of the oldest truths in the American story: We are not the subjects of kings or merely consumers of politics; we are citizens, the cocreators of a shared destiny.

The call of citizenship is not abstract. It begins in the daily practice of showing up for our community and for our country, by giving something back, listening, organizing, and building. This is the quiet work through which hope takes form.

In these chapters, we'll explore the journey of renewal. We will look honestly at what lives in our hearts and consider a question: Will we act as Subjects, Consumers, or Citizens? And we'll reflect on the truth that the bridge between our inner lives and the society we build is the place where democracy is either lost or reborn.

Here, citizenship becomes a verb. We learn how previous movements succeed, how victories are sustained, and how the moral imagination of a people can be rekindled through the shared work.

And we'll see that transformation never starts with everyone. Democratic renewal requires only *enough* of us. As history shows, small bands of determined people can awaken a nation and transform its nature. This is where the path turns from fear to courage, from isolation to solidarity, from exhaustion to purpose.

5

We must renew citizenship every
day through action, thought, and
participation.

—ELEANOR ROOSEVELT

The consumer is necessarily
passive; the citizen is necessarily
active.

—WENDELL BERRY

Subject, Consumer, or Citizen?

*The Stories Governments Tell
and the Choice Each of Us Faces*

My friend Bob is a hero, at least to me. I told him this once, and
he literally backed up, looked down, and shook his head. "No
way," he protested. "I am in no way a hero." I was praising Bob
for his years of volunteer work with an organization called
Family Promise, dedicated to preventing and ending family
homelessness.

I realized later that a better word for Bob, a more accurate one that he is far more apt to claim, is *Citizen.* By that, I mean someone who takes responsibility for his community rather than leaving it to others. His story shows us what that looks like, and the frequent smile on his face shows its result for him personally.

Now at retirement age, Bob began volunteering for Family Promise fifteen years ago. The families the organization supports stay at local churches for periods of time while they receive counseling and other forms of support. On behalf of his church, Bob organizes the dinner makers, unlocks the doors, inflates and makes the beds, and makes sure every family has a place to sleep. He oversees the cleanup, too, washing linens if others can't do it, packing away supplies, and staying overnight when needed.

For Bob, it doesn't feel one-sided or like a tedious chore. Far from it. "It's a two-way street," he says. "I get a lot back. I'm amazed at the character of the women who head these families and what it takes to hold things together. I admire their strength, and I feed off that strength. We feed them, and they feed us."

Bob feels a deep kinship with these families. "I feel that homelessness could have been my circumstance," he says. "I relate to people who live close to the edge. These are my kind of people. It delights me to help them."

Bob isn't my only hero. Sarah is one, too. She's 15 years old. Sarah proves that you don't even have to be old enough to vote to do the work our country needs.

At age 10, during the COVID lockdown, Sarah learned that four girls in a local homeless shelter might not have birthday cakes. She baked cakes for each of them and has continued baking to support the shelter's program ever since.

When I heard Sarah's story, I reached out to her mom with an idea: Since I'm an artist as well as a writer, how about the three of us put up an art show featuring my paintings of desserts alongside her cakes? Her mother, Amy, created a beautiful opening reception. People ate Sarah's cake and made contributions to Family Promise. We sold a lot of paintings. We raised a good bit of money, and we all learned how creativity and compassion can multiply and be a lot of fun.

Bob's and Sarah's stories remind me that citizenship goes far beyond voting. It's about the ways we choose to show up for one another, whether through supporting a homeless family, baking a cake, or lending a hand. Citizenship is far more than a legal status and not a garment we slip off when it grows uncomfortable. Further, unless we renounce it, citizenship is a bond we cannot escape. Whether we recognize it or not, to live in America is to be in constant relation to our country.

THE CHOICE TO BE A CITIZEN

A while back, I discovered a book, *Citizens* by Jon Alexander that changed my conception of what the word means. Alexander's book summarizes the three stories governments tell the governed about who they are. We can buy into these stories—or not. As you hear each one, ask yourself, which story do I find most compelling? Which role do I currently play?

One story says you are a passive *Subject*, that your job is principally to obey, another that you are to be a self-absorbed *Consumer*, and the third tells you that you are an active *Citizen*.

Only one of these stories lines up with what the Founders of America said democracy required.

Societies tend to organize themselves around how individuals see themselves; the *inner state* shapes the *outer system*. When people feel powerless, they accept subjugation and take on the role of Subject. When they mainly seek personal security or advantage, markets define their worth, and they assume the role of Consumer. But when they awaken to shared agency and purpose, they step into the Citizen role, and democracy flourishes.

Bob and Sarah both made the decision to be Citizens. I assert that America's future will be determined by how many of the rest of us step up to the *Citizen* role. (Throughout this chapter, I am going to capitalize that word to emphasize its importance.)

THE SUBJECT STORY

The Subject Story is told by the monarch, the autocrat, and the dictator. America's early colonists heard this story every day from King George, but some, about a third of the colonists and all those who signed the Declaration of Independence, didn't like it much. They didn't see themselves as the passive and dependent people the King said they should be. They didn't like it much when the King's soldiers claimed the right to invade their homes without a warrant, impose draconian taxes, and force them into military service.

The Subject Story tells you that you are expected to obey. Society under this story is hierarchical, with rulers, elites, or religious institutions at the top and everyone else at the bottom. What motivates individuals in this story is loyalty, duty, and fear of punishment.

In the Subject Story, rulers present themselves as strongmen—and almost always, governments that tell this story are led by males. Leaders across history sometimes reach for the tools of the strongman, even in democracies. Are we seeing this today? Consider these actions: Declaring sweeping emergencies, sidelining independent checks on power, disparaging cultural institutions, harassing universities, creating independent militias. When these tools are used, the relationship between leaders and the public starts to look less like what would be expected in a modern republic and more like the old Subject Story.

One terrible consequence of the Subject Story is that people's voices and creativity are suppressed. As this happens, society becomes rigid and less innovative. We touched on this when we spoke of the pre–Civil War South and Russia today. All forms of progress slow to a crawl or cease altogether when the Subject Story prevails. Innovation dries up. People have very little power to be who they are, and they have to watch what they say. As we explored earlier, this is the type of government some powerful extremists want for us again—male-dominated, unequal, despotic, run by a ruler. Will *We the People* stand for this?

In uncertain, stressful times, the Subject Story appeals to large numbers of people. A recent study found causal evidence that when people perceive societal breakdown, they tend to feel politically powerless and anxious, which in turn increases support for authoritarian leaders. When a populace is stressed with social and economic dislocations, polarization, extremism, and increasing political violence—as is true in America today—many wish for a strongman to sweep in and save the day, even if we have to trade our liberties for this. An article summarizing the study pointed to a predictable process in which breakdown "leads people to feel politically powerless, which then creates political uncertainty, ultimately increasing the appeal of authoritarian rule."[46]

THE CONSUMER STORY

The Consumer Story is entirely different and thoroughly modern. It is the predominant ethos in which we now live. It shapes how we think about nearly everything. We have built a society in which we are told that our primary role in life is to consume, that our worth is measured by what we buy, and that government exists to deliver the services we demand. It's a seductive narrative, but a hollow one. Jon Alexander states it starkly. "The Consumer Story goes like this: each of us is out for ourselves...Our task is to earn money, spend it, and compete with one another to climb society's ladder."

This story arose after WWII and was nurtured by the simultaneous rise of marketing, advertising, and mass production. Key to this story is the perception that we are distinct from one another. We are separate units, this story tells us, and our job is to compete with one another—for status, money, goods, and everything else. As Alexander puts it, "We have an epidemic of loneliness and mental health challenges, yet the story tells us we stand alone." In this story, the key to fixing anything is individual: Pull yourself up by your bootstraps. Leave the big problems to us." But who is us?

The tragedy of this story is that when people are primed to think of themselves as *consumers* rather than *citizens*, their motivation to engage in community, to care for neighbors, or to participate in collective life diminishes.

Some of us who are old enough remember a runaway bestseller that came out in 1977, shortly after America's social capital apex was reached. With a title that tells the Consumer Story like nothing else, it was called *Looking Out For #1*. In the book, author Robert Ringer, real-estate investor turned motivational author and lecturer, said, "Looking out for number one is the conscious effort to make rational decisions that lead to the greatest amount of happiness over the long term." And, lest we fear becoming lonely in the pursuit of happiness, he reassures us by saying, "Can you buy friendship? You not only can, you must. It's the only way to obtain friends. Everything worthwhile has a price."

As governments treat citizens as customers who consume services, rather than as participants who share responsibility for governing, we become passive and are encouraged subtly to demand and complain rather than get involved in cocreating our government. Civic life becomes a matter of "getting my needs met" instead of engaging in collective problem-solving.

This story reduces us to isolated economic actors chasing material comfort when what we truly need is trust and connection. Even our social relationships begin to feel transactional—what's in it for me? Meanwhile, we feel a strange malaise.

We're longing for something. What is it? It sure isn't advertising: We're bombarded minute by minute with advertising: on screens, in traffic, in our feeds. And what are we seeing in those ads? Things that others seem to have. The result is comparison, envy, and a quiet, constant sense of inadequacy.

In the Consumer Story, politicians see voters as buyers and present themselves as products in the marketplace. Once elected, however, those politicians largely ignore the needs of those who put them in office. Their primary concern is getting reelected. As this model takes root, the number of voters showing up diminishes. Today, politics has drifted far from the ideal of reasoned debate about what's best for our country. It has become a marketing enterprise, with candidates spending staggering sums less to persuade citizens than to raise still more money. When we contribute, our "thank you" is an endless stream of emails, texts, and ads that treat us not as partners in democracy but as targets.

The Consumer Story says, "Stay home, stay distracted, let others handle the big questions. Buy, buy, buy. Measure your worth by possessions and 'likes,' not by participation in shaping the common good. Retreat into smaller and smaller identity or market niches, rather than building coalitions across difference." Over time, consuming dulls our capacity for deeper satisfaction, the kind that comes from connection, purpose, and collective achievement.

Speaking candidly, the Consumer Story leaves me feeling empty and dispirited. How about you?

THE CITIZEN STORY

The Citizen Story offers a hopeful alternative. It calls us to be active, creative contributors to our neighborhoods, communities, and our country. It calls us to see citizenship not as a legal status but as a daily practice and a contribution. This is what the Founders called us to be and what we used to be. It's time to return to first principles.

Let me show you what the Citizen Story looks like in practice. In this case, the neighbors didn't get everything they wanted, but they did what the Founders of our country hoped citizens would do: they organized, they spoke up, and they learned along the way.

It began three years ago when Judith and her neighbors awoke to the sound of heavy machinery demolishing a house on their street. Shock turned to dismay when they discovered this modest home would be replaced by one nearly twice the size. Soon another house came down across the street. Neighbors learned that zoning codes had changed quietly, allowing oversized development that threatened the character of their neighborhood and the shade trees that gave the street its charm.

Alarmed, Judith gathered some of her neighbors and they began learning what they could do to preserve the nature of their neighborhood. The group contacted their township commissioner, met with planning staff, and attended council meetings. They proposed designating their block as a preservation zone. To make it happen, they needed majority support from the neighborhood, a goal that proved elusive. Some residents insisted they should be free to do whatever they wanted with property they owned, the trees be damned. Officials were sympathetic with their aims but inconsistent in following through. The goal is still unreached, yet Judith and her group remain hopeful, and their persistence moved township staff to take the idea seriously, something that would never have happened had they stayed silent.

Looking back, Judith was candid when she spoke to me about this. "I have no regrets about taking part in this process, but I do wish we had gone about it differently," she said. "We didn't know how to build support." Even so, she believes they achieved something important. "We pushed government to show flexibility and to open up to citizen influence. It took a lot of effort with uncertain results, but we all learned a lot." Some neighbors treated the group rudely, but many more were kind. "In the end, I'm glad I did it," she said.

Power in the Citizen Story is driven by a conviction: *We're all in this together.* Power arises from purpose, belonging, and contribution. When we take on the mantle of Citizen, we don't wait for someone above us to decide what our neighborhood, or community, or country should be. When *We the People* act as citizens, government begins to work for us, not the other way around.

Citizen energy shows up in many forms: volunteer fire companies, church-run food ministries, habitat builds, veterans' posts, youth sports, neighborhood watches, union halls, small-business associations, and mutual-aid networks. Different on the surface, they all practice the same habit, namely, showing up for one another. The Citizen Story represents a transformative possibility, the renewal of civic life rooted in cooperation and shared responsibility. Of the three stories, only this one offers agency and belonging.

When Thomas Jefferson wrote the Declaration of Independence, he created something the world had rarely seen before: Citizens rather than subjects. As historian and filmmaker Ken Burns observed, "Everybody heretofore has been subject to an authoritarian rule... And we've created a new thing called citizens." The Citizen Story is woven into our nation's beginnings and shows itself throughout our history.

Every reform that has advanced liberty was driven by citizens acting together.

Early Americans saw voting, staying informed, holding officials accountable, and showing up at meetings not as a grim duty but as a shared practice. But as we entered the twenty-first century, technology and modern life has made it harder to stay in Citizen mode. If television began pulling us away from civic life in the 1950s, the digital age has nearly severed that bond. Today, many see participation as impossible to fit into their busy lives or, worse, as someone else's job.

That we've fallen short of those ideals is not a failure of character but a consequence of systems that reward passivity and self-interest. The Citizen mentality hasn't vanished; it's been crowded out. Yet the health of democracy depends on reviving it, by choosing to act, to create, and to sustain the communities that make collective life possible.

RECLAIMING THE CITIZEN ROLE:
SOME THOUGHTS ON POWER

If we fail to reclaim the Citizen role, we will continue to face a host of ills: political gridlock, authoritarian drift, wealth inequality, and the loneliness/loss of purpose epidemic. Take heart. Reclaiming the Citizen role doesn't require heroism, extraordinary effort, or even devoting oneself to political activism. Fulfilling this role provides meaningful personal benefits as we connect with neighbors, discover a deeper sense of belonging, and experience the satisfaction of contributing to something larger than ourselves. This isn't just rah-rah boosterism; reams of psychological research support the personal benefits of connecting more deeply with others, aligning with a higher purpose, and supporting others.

Acting as a Citizen can take many forms: attending the PTA, taking on a *leadership* role in the PTA, or just volunteering for community projects. Citizens use the levers they already possess: Certainly voting, but also bringing one's knowledge, talents, and skills to efforts to sustain and build neighborhoods and communities. When enough people take even modest steps, the impact can multiply, enabling even small groups to reshape institutions, norms, and expectations. In Chapter Seven, we'll learn how small groups of determined citizens, acting in concert and over time, can create massive change. Indeed, this is the story of our history. Every corrective era in American life has begun not in the halls of power but in the hearts and actions of citizens working together to effect change. Politicians may give reforms their shape, but *citizens* get them to do so.

Next, I offer short stories about people that have decided to stop being Consumers and instead to act like Citizens. These are people who, in very different ways, are joining with others to make their part of the country better and, in the process, tell me they enjoy their own lives more as a result. I like the metaphor of lighting fires, the subject of Chapter Nine. By this I'm referring to actions ordinary Citizens take to make things better.

When it comes to building community, upon which democracy thrives, no action is insignificant. Some of us light a candle, some have the time and energy to light a torch, some of us light veritable bonfires. Each of us matters.

Light a Candle

Carol lit a candle when the regional rail system in her area was threatened by a state budget fight. She realized that a discontinuation of the trains would strand many hourly workers like her who depend on it to get to work and, further, would threaten local property values. She connected with a local citizens group that was fighting back and got ahold of some flyers. Contrary to her introverted nature, she put those flyers on windshields of cars in the parking lots of several stations and summoned the courage to speak with commuters who were boarding trains on a few days. Many had no idea the trains were threatened. Her effort didn't make all the difference, but she felt like she did something to preserve an important community resource and she made some new friends.

Fiona lives in a small apartment complex. The candle she lights comes in the form of periodic collections of plastics that a local company uses to upcycle into outdoor furniture. She says many people participate because they're glad not to have these plastics going into the trash stream. She goes door-to-door advertising and explaining the collections. As she does this, she meets and gets to know her neighbors. Occasionally, she learns of a need one has and makes a connection with another who can meet that need.

Light a Torch

Fran describes her service as "a candle," though when I listen to her, it feels more like a torch because of the extent of her commitment and the difference it makes. Fran spent much of her career as a chemistry professor and senior administrator at a distinguished college. She was careful to point out to me that she knows her life has been privileged and that awareness has become central to her story.

Every Wednesday, Fran spends two hours at a homeless shelter in a big city. I know that city; by the time she gets downtown, does her volunteer work, and gets back home, it's almost an entire day. She works behind the counter serving hot meals and cleaning up afterward. I asked her to put me in the room. "Anyone can walk in off the street and get food," she explains. "Many of the guests smell badly, some are high. But the shelter is an inspiration because it helps people. Some of the staff used to be homeless themselves."

I asked how she feels when the work is done, and she answered without hesitation. "I feel like I've made a contribution." But she paused and said, "Then I feel anger. When I think about all the wealth in this world and the people who are getting more wealthy by the day but hunger persists, it makes me crazy."

Why does she keep showing up, I asked her. "Because I see tremendous need. I grew up in the city. I've seen homeless my whole life. I feel horrible imagining what it would be like to live on the street—in the bitter cold, sitting on a vent. I used to say to my students, 'Here we are on this bucolic campus, but you don't have to go far to see people who are really impoverished. We think we have issues. Chemistry is hard. But the people who attend this college don't have problems, not really—we're privileged. But just a mile away from us people are living on the streets.'"

I told Fran that over the course of our conversation, her energy increased as she spoke. She laughed and said, "If I can make someone smile, maybe that produces grace. That's why I do this. Doing this fills me with energy."

Light a Bonfire

David never imagined himself to be a politician. He was a musician, not a lawyer, and activism had always felt less like a hunger and more like a duty. But in 2019, when he was 30 years old, Trump entered the White House for the first time, and he felt angry. A friend in Democratic politics challenged him by saying, "You have a lot of passion about this. You could be doing more with it."

David dove into volunteering for a local candidate, giving thirty hours a week while still holding a full-time job. He was good at managing, and ultimately, the candidate asked him to run the whole campaign. It was a trial by fire, but he learned how to do it. They didn't win, but three years later, angry about January 6 and disillusioned by his own party's inertia, he decided to enter a primary and run for office himself. His opponent had held the seat since David was in preschool and barely bothered to campaign each cycle.

Against the odds and after a great deal of effort, David won his party's endorsement with two-thirds of the vote, an unheard-of victory that made headlines. But the party's committee people, fearful of challenging the incumbent, refused to work for him. He lost the primary.

It was a bitter pill, but David insists it wasn't a failure. The run gave him visibility, deepened his ties to neighbors, and pressured his opponent to be more accountable. "Don't be discouraged by short-term setbacks," he encouraged me to tell others. "Impact matters more than victory. Sometimes losing today sets the stage for a win tomorrow."

His advice is clear: "In a lot of places, there is a desperation for candidates, especially for municipal and county level offices. This is true all over the country," he says. "Remember that you don't need to be an insider to run. Finally, keep in mind that you can do this."

David made clear to me that the real point of running for office isn't winning at all. It's taking responsibility, showing up, engaging your community, and refusing to let democracy run on autopilot. In other words, the point is to be a Citizen.

This chapter asked you to look at the stories you've absorbed about who you are in public life. Here's reality: You already practice one of these identities every day. The way you pay attention, spend money, speak up, or stay silent reinforce a role. Your power begins with choosing the role that aligns with the person you want to be. You are not stuck as a subject or a consumer. You can choose to act as a citizen.

STEPPING INTO YOUR POWER

So, here's the question: Which story *do* you live? Which story *will* you live?

The Citizen Story is demanding, especially when we feel cynical about government and politicians or have little time. But that difficulty is what can make it meaningful.

You may think, as I do, that our democracy needs renewal. If so, you might know that every great democratic renewal has come when ordinary people embraced the need for it, demanded it. We've done this throughout our history. If you are tired of division and discord and if your politics are not extreme, you are not alone by any means; you are in the majority. Will you get involved, if not in political activism, in something that strengthens your neighborhood or your community?

You may doubt whether your individual actions matter, especially in a country as large and divided as ours. I've felt that doubt myself. But personal power rarely announces itself with fanfare; it grows when we decide to take responsibility for even one small corner of our shared life. Every movement that ever strengthened American democracy began with people who felt ordinary, unsure, or skeptical—and who acted anyway.

In the next chapter, we'll turn our attention to the future—or, more precisely, to the generation that will inherit this democracy and decide what it becomes. Perhaps you count yourself among them. Or perhaps, like me, you are older, looking toward those who come after us with equal measures of hope and concern. If we want to be effective partners in strengthening what they will receive, we must understand their world, their challenges, and their aspirations more deeply. Only then can we support them in ways that matter, helping them build a future worthy of their inheritance.

KEY IDEAS IN THIS CHAPTER

* We live inside competing stories: *The Subject Story* demands obedience to authority. *The Consumer Story* trains us to be spectators and shoppers. *The Citizen Story* invites participation, contribution, and shared purpose.

* Citizenship is active, not passive. It's about voting, but also showing up—helping neighbors, strengthening community, and taking shared responsibility.
* The Citizen Story restores meaning, belonging, and agency. It reminds us that power grows through connection and collaboration.
* Democracy mirrors its citizens' psychology. When fear rules hearts, nations grow brittle; when courage and compassion prevail, democracy heals.
* Ordinary people sustain democracy. Whether lighting a candle, a torch, or a bonfire, every act of civic participation strengthens the whole.

6

Sudden change is possible, and the youth must force it.

—SAUL ALINSKY, ORGANIZER AND ACTIVIST

The future belongs to those who give the next generation reason for hope.

—PIERRE TEILHARD DE CHARDIN, JESUIT PRIEST AND INTELLECTUAL

The Inheritors

The Crucial Role of the Young in Reclaiming Democracy

This past summer, while sitting on a beach talking to a contemporary (we're both in our late 70s) about the subject of this book, we agreed that we're leaving our offspring and their generation with a mess. I said, "I feel like going around to all the young people on this beach right now and apologizing!" So, I'll say this to every young person reading this book: My generation didn't solve our problems, and we made many worse. We need you, and we'll stand with you to make things better.

Let me speak directly. I am asking you, Americans aged 18–40, to engage with and fix a political system that often offends you for its inefficiency, deceit, and tawdriness. I know that sounds contradictory and is a lot to ask—get busy fixing a system that you disdain—and it is. But here's why it matters. Unless you get involved in protecting democracy from the risks to core democratic norms, your opportunity to enable that restructuring goes up in smoke. I don't mean to induce guilt. I'm just trying to be real about the consequences.

Will you step in for America by organizing, voting, building, and serving? This is more than a rhetorical question. one in five of Americans 18–45 are actively planning to leave the country to live abroad. If you've considered leaving, I understand. But I hope you'll stay and help shape the country you want to live in.

TOM'S STORY

I'm not sure Tom is onboard.

Tom, a 31-year-old electrician, told me that he thinks America's problems go beyond lost trust in institutions—he believes the social contract itself has crumbled. "We used to have this unwritten agreement," he said, "that in exchange for our taxes, government would provide services for the people. That started to unravel," he said, "when they dismantled the programs of the New Deal. Then, it was Reagan deregulation. Citizens United finished the job."

Tom is a registered Democrat but calls himself a Democratic Socialist, not because he wants revolution, but because, as he put it, "it's a tool for helping the average person, to make life more comfortable and secure." He doesn't fit neatly into any political category. He supports the Second Amendment, distrusts both major parties, and believes we should rewrite the Bill of Rights for the twenty-first century to include food, housing, healthcare, and water as human rights.

Tom came to hold these views when he watched the 2008 Recession unfold while in high school. He told me how a video stuck with him: It showed unemployed people lining up for unemployment benefits while Wall Street traders jeered at them and called them losers. "That clip changed me," he said. "It showed what kind of society we'd become." Obama's election gave him hope, he said, but by the end of that presidency, Tom saw something different taking root, saying, "The racism it unleashed, the cynicism that followed—it all felt like a turning for the worst."

Tom doesn't feel either party represents him and he sees politics as filled with hypocrisy. "The Democrats and Republicans are two sides of the same coin," he said. "They've both let money corrupt them. Republicans complain about George Soros putting too much money in politics, then Elon Musk does the same thing."

Like many in his generation, Tom lives under the weight of economic anxiety and was open about this. He told me, "All of my friends are getting financial help from their parents—for car payments, down payments, health insurance." At the same time, he said, young people "are consuming like there's no tomorrow. Because there doesn't seem to *be* a tomorrow." Tom wonders if he'll ever be able to afford a home.

Still, Tom hasn't given up. He votes, though admitting, "My vote doesn't change anything." I challenged him: "Why vote if it changes nothing?" He replied quickly, "I do it because it's my civic duty." What gives him hope are new voices, people like Zohran Mamdani and the "No Kings" demonstrators, who have shown him that ordinary Americans can still make themselves heard. He acknowledges that his support for the Second Amendment puts him at odds with many of the people trying to effect change today but says, "Even if I don't agree with half of those No Kings marchers, I'm proud they're showing up."

At the end of our conversation, I told Tom I was impressed by his clarity and decency, his love for our country. He didn't shrug it off or turn self-conscious. He simply said, "I had a good education." When I asked what that meant to him, he said something that stayed with me. "I went to good public schools. I did go to college. This taught me to form arguments and speak my mind effectively, to have conversations with people who see things differently, and to offer a respectful rebuttal without suppressing what they've said." Hearing this moved me and uplifted me. I told him that this is the essence of what it means to be a good citizen.

YOUNG VOTERS THROUGH THE MICROSCOPE

If the young are the hinge on which this republic swings, who are they?

Let's say the young are people of voting age up to 40. This is a bloc that has potential clout: Younger voters' influence is expanding, especially in key battleground states, since elections are often decided by turnout in precisely those groups. By recent estimates, this group now makes up more than 30 percent of all eligible voters, but just over half of them voted in 2024 and far fewer vote in midterm and off-year elections.

What do these young voters believe? Recalling that pluralism refers to a system in which multiple groups, beliefs, values, or identities coexist and share power within the same society, how do younger voters feel about the importance of defending it? How do they regard the two political parties? What actions are they taking in support of their views? And if they aren't doing much politically, why not?

Those in this cohort do not usually think of themselves in political terms, and their political views are far less rigid than others who wear their party affiliation on their sleeves. Consequently, many in this age group identify as independents, contributing to a political sea-change underway; the 2024 election marked a high point for independent identification. Self-identified independents outnumbered Democrats and were equal with Republicans, representing the largest share of independents in modern polling, according to some sources.[47]

On the topic of democracy, Gen Z attitudes, i.e., voters aged 18–28, will give pause to anyone who cares about the future of democracy. While most Americans, across party lines affirm a strong commitment to democracy and the Constitution (three-quarters say the Constitution deserves wide respect for the stability it provides, and roughly two-thirds of Americans believe democracy is "definitely the best" form of government), this consensus weakens sharply among Gen Zers.[48]

In a More in Common 2025 study, a quarter of young Americans say they don't really care about the Constitution, and only about four in ten Gen Z respondents said they believe democracy is clearly the best system. Even more concerning, nearly half of Gen Z respondents said it can be acceptable for leaders to set aside democratic principles to fix the economy—far higher than when a respondent identified with either political party. While older generations largely uphold democratic norms, many younger Americans express ambivalence about democracy's value, particularly when weighed against their economic concerns.[49]

This population of Americans is deeply disillusioned; many are convinced that their voices and priorities are routinely ignored. For Gen Zers, partisan warfare, gridlock, and unresponsive political elites reinforce the sense that democracy simply isn't delivering. As a result, voting feels pointless to many of them. One study found that an astonishing 90 percent of voters under 40 described themselves as frustrated or angry with politicians in Washington, and another reported that three-quarters of all respondents believe elected officials primarily serve the wealthy.[50]

This level of cynicism carries troubling consequences. When young Americans come to believe their voices don't matter and that politicians answer only to the powerful, voting no longer feels like a meaningful act. Their disillusionment is a warning signal: When a government fails to deliver for the rising generation, it cannot count on their continued participation in democracy.

On the value of pluralism, the picture for younger voters is mixed. On the one hand, young Americans generally support LGBTQ+ rights, same-sex marriage, transvestitism, gender fluidity, and religious plurality. But while these freedom lovers want to see legal protections in these areas and are far more racially tolerant than my generation generally is, some research suggests that tolerant individuals only mobilize under favorable conditions; their broad support does not automatically trigger activism, especially when structural or social costs are high.[51]

In key issue areas like LGBTQ+ and ecological concerns, some in this cohort are engaged but most are not. Even voting by the group is episodic. Sadly, many do not believe that involvement in politics will help them improve their lives. A majority of this age group feels that contacting elected officials or attending rallies is ineffective.[52]

The 18–40 age group is left-leaning, but they have little to no confidence in either political party to solve problems. Who can blame them? In their lifetimes, they've seen the parties produce little but rancor. Many younger voters regard both parties with contempt, convinced that politicians are consumed by self-interest and blind to the realities of their generation. (They're hardly alone. In a devastating indictment, 65 percent of adults say that all or most people who seek office do so to serve their own personal interests, while just 21 percent say they do so to serve their communities.[53])

All this leads to distrust in government. According to a 2025 Harvard Youth Poll, only 19 percent of young people said they trust the federal government to do the right thing "most or all the time." Confidence is even lower for Congress (18 percent), but not much higher for the presidency (23 percent) and the Supreme Court (29 percent).[54]

GEN Z AND CHRISTIAN NATIONALISM

The Christian right faces a dilemma. Should they accept their minority status and stay with the strategy of using their high turnout advantage to advance their cause or find nondemocratic means to gain ground? Increasingly, forces on the right find the latter attractive. So do a lot of Gen Z voters.

Writing in the *New York Times,* Daniel Williams, associate professor of history at Ashland University, says, "In the aftermath of Covid—and amid the longing for purpose, community and transcendence that many Gen Zers feel—a sizable minority of them have found their answer in conservative Christianity, fueling both a religious and a political revival among these young Americans."[55]

Not surprisingly, Professor Williams observes that many in Gen Z—especially males—are drawn to Charlie Kirk's message of "spiritual warfare," a term Kirk used repeatedly in his later speeches and at Turning Point Faith events. Kirk associated the term with the idea that American politics and culture represent a struggle between divine and demonic forces. (Donald Trump has also referred to himself as a "spiritual warrior," as has Secretary of Defense, Pete Hegseth.) Young males outnumber females at Turning Point Faith events. The brand of Christianity these Gen Z worshipers find most attractive tends to be anti-institutional and led by strong, charismatic men.

SEEDS OF RENEWAL—AND REASON FOR CONCERN—IN A RESTLESS GENERATION

Though distrustful, Gen Z voters remain one of the most motivated cohorts in American life—proof that civic energy still stirs beneath the surface of disconnection.

1. Sixty-seven percent of Gen Z oppose all Project 2025 conservative policy proposals (vs. 61 percent of all voters).

2. Gen Z conservatives tend to be disproportionately male and religious, while Gen Z liberals are more often female and college-educated—a deep internal divide within the generation.

3. Gen Zers are "news receivers," not "news seekers": Only 38 percent say they actively seek news, while 61 percent said they mostly "bump into it." As voters age, they seek news more often. Gen Zers bump into news via social media.

4. Perhaps reflecting this, exit polls in the 2025 election show that women aged 30 and under voted over 80 percent for Mamdani, Sherill, and Spanberger. Males in that cohort lagged behind but were also generally supportive: 67 percent for Mamdani and 58 percent for Sherill and Spanberge (NBC News).

5. Alarmingly, 56 percent of Gen Z say violence against elected officials may sometimes be justified—the highest among all generations. 57 percent see public disruption and 41 percent see destruction of property as valid protest forms.

Source unless otherwise indicated: Bipartisan Policy Center's Citizen Data

FOR MANY YOUNG VOTERS, SOCIALISM IS NOT A DIRTY WORD

For Americans under 40, socialism has far more appeal than it does with older generations who readily conflate it with communism. A March 2025 survey by Cato Institute, in partnership with YouGov, found that 62 percent of Americans ages 18–29 say they hold a "favorable view" of socialism. Millennials and Gen Zers are also significantly more likely than Baby Boomers to believe that capitalism has serious flaws.[56]

What young people mean by "socialism" is often different from any textbook definition. For Gen Zers and Millennials, the word signals something closer to universal healthcare, affordable housing, student debt relief, and fair wages than state control of industry. The openness among younger voters to socialism is less about abolishing markets and more about ensuring security, fairness, and dignity in an economy they see as rigged against ordinary people. To this age group, socialism, with its promise of fairness and equity, seems worth exploring.

This openness is fueled by lived experience. Younger Americans face steep housing costs, burdensome student loans, and stagnant wages. They have also come of age during financial crises and growing inequality, which makes capitalism seem less like a system of opportunity and more like one of deeply entrenched unfairness. For many, socialism does not represent an ideology so much as a potential corrective.

Support for socialism depends heavily on framing. Younger voters respond positively to proposals for free healthcare or tuition but far less positively when socialism is described in terms of government ownership or centralized control. Views also diverge sharply by party. Young Democrats lean heavily in favor, while young Republicans remain skeptical.

Tom's story aligns with this. On this topic he said, "To me, socialism is not a scary word. To me, it's a tool for helping the average person, to make life more comfortable and secure. I am not afraid of this word at all."

Why this matters is that younger Americans are reshaping the debate over the type of economic system we should have. Their views are a reflection of generational pressure points. For politicians on the left, younger voters' openness to socialism is both an opportunity and a challenge. It gives them room to push bold reforms on issues like healthcare, housing, wages, and climate, but it also demands careful framing: emphasizing fairness and practical solutions rather than ideology. Millennials and Gen Z, voting blocs with increasing clout as Boomers die out, expect leaders to address their economic struggles and to treat activism as part of politics, not as noise on the sidelines. Those who tap into this energy can shape the agenda for decades, while those who dismiss it risk appearing out of touch and losing a generation of voters.

WHY ARE YOUNGER AMERICANS DISENGAGED?

There are many reasons why younger voters are disengaged. The interviews I conducted for this book confirm this, as does recent research.

One reason has to do with how they think. Young Americans have grown up with systems thinking; they see problems systemically. They understand that climate change, inequality, and democratic backsliding are interconnected. But electoral politics forces them into the restrictive frame of competing individual candidates whose policy proposals seem superficial. When you believe the entire system needs restructuring, voting for someone who promises to tinker at the edges feels more than inadequate.

Politics for younger voters is anathema because, more than older voters, digital natives expect transparency. Where older voters tolerate scripted messaging, younger ones see manipulation—and despise it. Their disillusionment isn't cynicism; it's pattern recognition. Which raises the question:

Their worldview is also global. They think beyond local, state, and federal boundaries, viewing issues like climate change and inequality as challenges that transcend borders. Asked whether they feel more like citizens of the world or of the United States, many say the former.

Another reason younger voters are disengaged has to do with the continual disruption our times represent. Older Americans like me grew up in a time where there were relatively long stretches of stability punctuated by brief crises. But today's young adults have known only disruption—childhoods marked by 9/11, adolescence during the 2008 financial collapse, early careers shaped by COVID, and now an adulthood dominated by Trump and shadowed by the perils of climate change and artificial intelligence.

Tom mentioned economic anxiety and noted that the old contract is broken. For many younger voters, education no longer guarantees homeownership or even stable work. Debt for many is crushing, and the system feels rigged. When Tom said, "there doesn't seem to *be* a tomorrow," he reflects this.

APPEALING TO THE YOUNG

Unfortunately for democracy, the best current example of an organization that appeals to younger voters is Turning Point USA (TPUSA). I say "unfortunately" because TPUSA, founded by

Charlie Kirk when he was 18, promotes antidemocratic values and is highly aligned with the values of Christian nationalism. It has been criticized by civil rights groups as racially divisive and maintains what can only be called a snitch list to identify and target left-leaning campus professors. Democracy lovers benefit, though, by understanding how this organization appeals to young voters.

TPUSA is very well endowed. In the year this is written (2025), it had revenue of about $85 million per year. That is a great deal of money for *any* nonprofit organization. TPUSA's funding comes mostly from contributions, gifts, and grants from conservative organizations.[57]

The potency of TPUSA comes from a simple, energizing story at its core: Members are underdogs fighting back against evil in the form of elite institutions, wokeism, invasion by immigrants, and moral decay. This gets supercharged by telling them their fight is sanctioned by God. This framing transforms isolation into pride and gives the organization a reach that many traditional political groups struggle to match.

TPUSA has built a very sophisticated, pop-culture brand that is reflected in memes, slogans, concerts, and merchandise that let students signal belonging as easily as wearing a T-shirt. Its website shows dazzling branding sophistication. With chapters on 800 campuses and in 1,000 high schools, TPUSA gives young conservatives an instant community in places where they often feel isolated. That network matters in a world where young people often struggle to find real community.

Compared with the scale and discipline of TPUSA, campus organizing on the left is far more diffuse and not nearly as well funded. Progressive groups often form around specific causes—civil rights, democratic socialism, reproductive justice, or Palestinian solidarity—rather than under one unified banner, as TPUSA does. College Democrats of America, the National Association for the Advancement of Colored People (NAACP) Youth & College Division, the Young Democratic Socialists of America, and Students for Justice in Palestine all have substantial footprints, but their efforts remain scattered, lacking coherence and clout. The result is an ecosystem that is passionate yet fragmented, rich in energy but without centralized power or shared branding.

Newer efforts, however, suggest that youth engagement is evolving. *The Next Gen Come Up*—founded by activist Anya Dillard when she was still a teenager—blends protest, community service, and art to empower young people as changemakers. Rejecting rigid partisan structures, it flourishes in social-media spaces, classrooms, and local neighborhoods, where civic action feels creative, relational, and personal. Its ethos embodies a generational shift toward a do-it-yourself, grassroots democracy built through belonging rather than bureaucracy.

At the institutional end of the spectrum is *NextGen America*, a well-funded national operation focused squarely on driving youth voting turnout. Founded by billionaire Tom Steyer, it deploys substantial resources in battleground states such as Arizona and Pennsylvania, registering millions of young voters and helping to shape progressive electoral outcomes.

Meanwhile, *March for Our Lives* stands as the moral voice of youth activism. Born after the Parkland school shooting, it built hundreds of chapters and led some of the largest demonstrations against gun violence in U.S. history. Its enduring power comes not from money but from authenticity and urgency.

Together, these movements reveal the left's generational tension: a landscape alive with creativity and conviction but lacking the centralized coordination that gives conservative counterparts their strategic coherence.

STEPPING INTO YOUR POWER

If you are under 40, I've been talking about you for many pages now. I hope you don't mind. People my age need to understand you better so we can stand alongside you.

So, I ask plainly: Will you defend our democracy? If you yearn for a better America, will you join with others to build it? The system is imperfect, even seriously flawed, yes, and offends you in many ways, but you have the chance to reshape it. You are America's greatest strength. Yours is a generation more diverse, more connected, more educated, and more committed to justice than any before. Every generation faces a defining test. This is yours. The tools of change are already in your hands: your vote, your voice, your energy, your networks, your platforms, your moral clarity.

If you're young, seeing yourself as an inheritor of unfinished work can feel daunting, but it can also be grounding. You are part of a long continuum of people who faced their moment and did what they could. Your power comes from recognizing that you stand in that line. You don't need to carry the whole weight of history, only the portion that falls to you.

And then, to all of us, young and old alike, a simple question: Will America be the birthright of a few or the common home of all? Will we be a nation that welcomes the stranger, as every great religious and moral tradition commands?

Young people will own the future, but change also arrives through the steady courage of small, committed groups made up of people of all ages.

Next, we explore the mathematics of hope: how even a few percent of engaged citizens, organized and persistent, can shift the course of a nation.

KEY IDEAS IN THIS CHAPTER

* Democracy's future rests with the under-40 cohort; disengagement by this group empowers a highly organized few who reject what they value.
* Younger voters aren't antidemocratic so much as disappointed by its performance; earning trust requires their involvement and making tangible gains.
* Meaning + community = mobilize: Movements win when they create the belonging, purpose, and identity every generation needs but Gen-Zs and Millennials lack.
* Politicians must meet the generation where it lives: fast feedback, transparent leadership, flexible on-ramps, and reforms that reward participation.
* The assignment for all ages is to match the far right's intensity with disciplined, pluralist organizing: Vote in all elections, build local power, and make sure the flag is a banner under which all people can stand.

7

Small Numbers, Big Change

How Small Numbers of People Can Drive Transformative Political Change

In a suburban township meeting on a cold autumn night, a hearing about leaf blowers drew people out of their homes to speak, question, challenge, and ultimately shape a policy that affected their lives.

I came because I wanted to see how *We the People* showed up, not how the vote turned out. I was reminded that the levers of democracy are still within reach, often closer than we think. I saw what democracy looked like that night: humans wrestling with change, fear, facts, identity, power, and one another. I saw how power was used and what it looks like when organized and when it isn't.

At issue was a potential ban on gas-powered leaf blowers, contentious in my area due to noise and pollution. On two earlier occasions the public had spoken, but this was voting night, so a large crowd gathered. Two local TV crews were present. When I arrived, I had to make my way past one of them. A reporter was interviewing a tiny boy speaking earnestly into the lights. Dressed in a crisp white shirt with neatly combed hair, he wasn't much taller than the reporter's waist but had the poise of an adult.

The president of the Board instructed speakers to state their name and address, and a long line formed. For more than two hours, over fifty people spoke. Glancing at the queue, I saw the little boy sandwiched between large men studying their notes.

A high school student in a t-shirt praised the Council's careful study: "Please pass this ban," he said, adding that opponents were good people who deserved to be heard. "Change is hard," he acknowledged.

Opponents warned that batteries for electric blowers were costly and short-lived—$100 each, then $200, then $300, then $400 as the evening wore on. Nearly every speaker, for or against, overstated their case. The ban would kill local businesses. Batteries posed fire hazards. Gas blowers caused Alzheimer's.

The small boy eventually reached the podium. Praising the commissioners, he read an eloquent statement about health hazards, then handed over a petition with one hundred signatures he collected from students at his school. We should all be citizens, like him, I thought.

He was followed by a landscaper in Carhartt work clothes. "Electric blowers are inferior," he said. "They cost more. They take too long to charge." Then, with emotion: "Gas blowers have been life-changing for me. What's next—chain saws? Mowers? What gives you the right to take away my freedom?"

Another landscaper said he supported cleaner equipment "in principle," but that "the technology isn't there yet," a phrase I'd hear many times that night. He estimated the ban would cost his business $100,000. "I've looked into it," he said.

The evening soon became a contest not only over blower types but over resources and preparation. Supporters of the ban—mostly retirees—brought coordination, research, citations, and polished remarks. Landscapers, many arriving straight from work, had none of this.

Retired doctors listed hazards hazards to residents: lethal exhaust, cognitive decline, autism, depression. Risks to the operators themselves, who likely bear the greatest exposure, received less emphasis.

As the evening wore on, the white-collar speakers clearly gained the upper hand, yet opposition remained passionate. A homeowner insisted, "The only way to move the amount of leaves we have is with a gas blower. Are you telling us we'll go to jail for using the only kind that works?"

A female landscaper testified that her business has been using electric blowers for nine years. She assured the Commissioners: "We've had no problems, no fires, and we're making money."

When I stepped out to stretch, she was speaking with the Carhartt landscaper who had opposed the ban. He asked her detailed questions about costs and maintenance. When he stepped away, I asked her how powerful the equipment really is. "We find it better than the gas blowers. Remember," she said, "We don't buy the equipment we use at Home Depot—it's professional grade." How much does a battery cost, and do they wear out quickly, as some have claimed, I asked her? She couldn't tell me the cost—they had never had to replace one in nine years.

A final speaker, a *New York Times* reporter deeply knowledgeable about the issue, delivered a polished account of hazards including hearing loss, toxins, and noise. Only later did I learn she had been recruited by the retirees.

Finally, before the vote, the commissioners had an opportunity to speak. The commissioner most responsible for bringing forth the ordinance compassionately acknowledged the difficulty of change. Another, addressing the fears about harsh legal penalties, reassured everyone that no contractor was going to jail for failing to comply. Other commissioners expressed their appreciation, in respectful ways for all who had taken the time to speak. Their understanding of the contractors' concerns struck me as respectful, empathic, and gracious. Experiencing their thoughtfulness and sincerity, I found myself with a deeper appreciation for my community.

The measure to phase out gas-powered blowers passed 10–4.

Driving home, it seemed to me that the process I had just witnessed was not flattering to anyone—doctors overstating risks, professionals dominating, contractors overstating costs and equipment limitations, the opposition failing to organize. But this is what democracy looks like. Human. Imperfect.

I realized that what I witnessed that night was more than a local quarrel about leaf blowers. It was a small reminder of a larger truth: Democratic life depends on ordinary people showing up, speaking up, and staying engaged, even when the issues are mundane and the process can be maddening. Most of the time, nothing dramatic happens—no sweeping reforms, no grand victories. And yet, these small acts of participation accumulate. They shape the norms, relationships, and expectations that determine how power moves in a community. They reveal how change actually happens.

Our democratic process isn't pretty. In the give and take, some people get their way and others don't. But all in all, *We the People* looked pretty good to me that night.

HOW SMALL GROUPS CREATE CHANGE

Most of the time, democracy looks modest or even chaotic, nothing like the dramatic turning points we read about in history books. But political scientists have found that this kind of small-scale engagement is precisely where deeper shifts start. The patterns I saw in that township meeting are the same ones that determine how meaningful change takes root in countries around the world when people seek it.

Chenoweth and Stephen analyzed over 323 campaigns around the world from 1900 to 2006. They found something remarkable: Change rarely requires a majority. In fact, even a small fraction of the population—sometimes as low as 3 percent–4 percent—can alter the direction of a nation when acting with cohesion and commitment over time.

What matters is not mass mobilization, but the presence of people who show up, who speak, who organize, who say: *This is our community, and we have a stake in it.* Their work reveals just how much impact small, determined groups of citizens can have and why the strategies that shaped our founding era still matter. If you've read this far, you likely share a desire to see our country change for the better. What these researchers have uncovered offers both a methodology and a hope.

Those who are familiar with this work find the central finding encouraging: Across more than a century of cases, Chenoweth and Stephen found that movements successful in mobilizing on the order of ≈3.5 percent of the population in sustained, nonviolent action *very often* succeed. This "threshold effect" as they call it is consistently the moment after which nonviolent movements achieve outsized leverage.

Here are examples from our own history:

The American Revolution. Here are examples from our own history: The truth this chapter explores is as American as apple pie. Consider this: American colonists had been preparing our country for independence well before shots were fired at Lexington and Concord in April 1775. Those early American patriots didn't wait for George Washington to save them; they took matters into their own hands.

By the time the American Revolution broke out, countless acts of civil resistance had already made the colonies nearly ungovernable. What's striking is that this transformation was driven by a relatively small portion of the population, ordinary people whose persistence made an extraordinary difference.

Civil Rights Movement. No one would call the Civil Rights Movement of the 1960s "small," but when you think about the absolute numbers of people involved compared to the U.S. population, it fits Chenoweth's model.

There's no single definitive number that captures all those involved, but the number of Americans participating almost certainly wasn't over 15 percent. The movement's success depended not just on visible leaders like Martin Luther King Jr. but crucially on the participation of enough ordinary people who risked jobs, safety, and even their lives and thus gained moral legitimacy.

The Civil Rights Movement is instructive in another way: the sheer variety of methods used, a requirement for effective movements as Chenoweth found. In *Civil Resistance,* she writes:

> The U.S. Civil Rights Movement...involved various forms of civil resistance—marches, bus boycotts, lunch counter sit-ins, consumer boycotts, silent processions, public prayer and worship, mass demonstrations, the deliberate overloading of jails, and many other methods—alongside more traditional political methods like issuing public statements, legal advocacy, lobbying the White House and congressional elites, and supporting antiracist candidates for public office.

Women's Suffrage Movement (1848–1920). The fight for women's suffrage was powered by decades of disciplined, nonviolent persistence. In church basements and town halls, teachers, mothers, and reformers organized petitions, marches, and public lectures that slowly reshaped the nation's moral imagination. They endured ridicule, arrest, and violence yet refused to abandon peaceful tactics. By 1920, the National American Woman Suffrage Association had roughly 2 million members—less than 2 percent of the U.S. population—and even with allies, participation remained well below 3.5 percent. Still, through sustained pressure and moral appeal, suffragists shifted the cultural pillars that upheld exclusion and won passage of the Nineteenth Amendment.

Labor Movement (early 1900s–1930s). The early labor movement, too, demonstrated how collective action from below can bend institutions above. Through strikes, boycotts, and walkouts, workers withdrew their cooperation from an economic order that treated them as expendable and exposed them to hostile working conditions. Factories went silent, trains stood idle, and the moral logic of unrestrained capitalism began to fracture. Crucially, the movement built alliances with journalists, clergy, and progressive reformers. The resulting political pressure led to the Fair Labor Standards Act, the eight-hour workday, and the right to organize. All this transformed not just workplaces but also the social contract itself.

Environmental Movement (1960s–1970s). A century later, the modern environmental movement began, following a similar playbook. It began not in legislatures but in living rooms, classrooms, and college campuses, where people gathered to discuss the warnings of Rachel Carson's *Silent Spring*. The first Earth Day in 1970 mobilized scientists, students, and suburban parents alike. Twenty million Americans in all were involved. This peaceful activism helped produce sweeping reforms, including the Clean Air Act, the Clean Water Act, and the creation of the Environmental Protection Agency. Once again, a small but visible minority forced a reckoning with the status quo through coordinated nonviolent action. There is plenty more work to do, but this is a story worth remembering.

Marriage Equality Movement (1990s–2015). The struggle for marriage equality has shown how moral persuasion, cultural storytelling, and disciplined legal advocacy can change hearts and how those changed hearts can drive changes in our laws. LGBTQ+ activists and their allies didn't seize power; they told stories of love, dignity, and belonging that softened public resistance. As families, churches, and communities began to defect from old prejudices, the political landscape shifted. When the Supreme Court finally recognized same-sex marriage in 2015, it was the culmination of decades of peaceful persistence that had normalized compassion and made equality not just legal but imaginable.

Each of these movements succeeded not by drawing on entrenched power, seizing power, or by using violence, but when individuals formed small groups and those groups joined together to enlarge the nation's moral imagination.

Groups like Indivisible represent a new wave of grassroots, prodemocracy organizations that empower ordinary people to participate meaningfully in public life. They blend digital organizing with action, helping volunteers gather in living rooms, libraries, and community centers to learn about issues, pressure lawmakers, and strengthen democratic norms.

An initiative called Courage Collectives, launched by Indivisible, begins with a simple but radical premise, upheld by the Chenoweth/Stephan research: Autocrats depend on the cooperation of the institutions that surround them—business, faith, education, the press, civil service, the military. When those pillars refuse to comply, the edifice of authoritarianism weakens. Courage Collectives invite citizens to organize within the communities they already belong to—teachers within schools, veterans within the armed forces, alumni within universities, congregants within churches—to help those institutions find their moral footing.

Many of these groups are often built around small local chapters yet are connected through shared tools, trainings, and messaging. They emphasize accountability, voter participation, and pluralism rather than ideological purity or partisan hostility. Similar organizations today, such as Swing Left, Common Cause, Braver Angels, Voters of Tomorrow, and the League of Women Voters, share this commitment to equipping everyday citizens with the skills, confidence, and community needed to influence elections, defend institutions, and practice the habits of citizenship together.

An example is a network of pastors in Washington State that is reclaiming the language of faith from political manipulation. Another is a group of educators in California who are organizing to resist censorship and defend the integrity of public education. Each effort is small, but together, they represent something larger: citizens remembering their agency, choosing courage over compliance.

POLITICAL INVOLVEMENT AS LONELINESS ANTIDOTE?

Some young Americans, evidently, are discovering that political engagement can be an antidote to cynicism—and, for some, a way to feel human again. When 34-year-old state legislator Zohran Mamdani launched his campaign for New York City mayor, he didn't just talk policy. Recognizing the deep loneliness and disconnection among younger voters, his team organized bar meet-ups, board-game nights, and post canvassing dinners. More than 100,000 volunteers eventually joined.

A *New York Times* reporter observed that many were emerging from what one volunteer called "post-pandemic drift." They described themselves as anxious, overworked, and lonely. What drew them in was not simply housing planks or transit plans, but the chance to belong. "It's honestly what I'd prescribe for the loneliness epidemic," one 28-year-old said.

Mamdani's campaign became an accidental case study in activism as social intervention. In the previous mayoral election, just over 11% of voters under 30 cast ballots; this time, more than 40% did. Engagement became a source of community: Volunteers built friendships, and organizing felt less like work and more like connection.

It paid off: more than 1 million New Yorkers voted for him, contributing to the highest turnout in a mayoral election in over fifty years.

STEPPING INTO YOUR POWER

This chapter reveals that successful change efforts don't need a majority. Change begins with small groups, sometimes very small ones, that stay focused long enough to make a difference. To make change, you don't need sweeping influence; you need a foothold and a handful of people who care as much as you do.

Every movement that has driven significant change in our country began as murmurs among people on the margins: women gathering in parlors, workers striking in factories, students marching on campuses, couples daring to speak their love aloud. This coalesced into a chorus that reshaped what America believed about itself. America's renewal, these historical examples remind us, almost never begins in the halls of government. It begins wherever ordinary people decide that the promise of freedom and liberty made at our founding must be fulfilled.

Ordinary people, working with others of varied backgrounds, occupations, and walks of life can make huge social change through nonviolent means—but only when they stay engaged. The hinge is engagement. When enough people choose to show up, especially those with time, resources, or influence, nonviolence, when coupled with a compelling message, scales.

Our country has deep problems. But even amid crises, there are practical avenues for action. We've learned in this chapter that a small percentage of active people can create history-making change. The future doesn't depend on getting everyone involved. It depends on you, and on the circles you build.

What if you were part of that 3.5 percent in America? What if you and a few million other ordinary Americans decided to act together? Sure, this would take time to build, but history shows that when small groups commit themselves to change, they win. The question isn't whether it can be done. The question is, Will *you* join them?

We now understand that democratic renewal begins with small groups acting with conviction and discipline. The next chapter turns theory into tools and shows how ordinary people and organizations are pushing forward and sustaining the change we urgently need.

KEY IDEAS IN THIS CHAPTER

* History isn't made only by elites or majorities; sustained, nonviolent action by a small percentage of a population can tip whole systems.
* Nonviolence succeeds because it invites broad coalitions, wins moral legitimacy, and pressures multiple "pillars" of power to stop cooperating.
* The American story began with citizens acting even before the Revolution; that civic muscle is still available to us.
* You don't need everyone—just enough committed people acting together over time. The question isn't *can* it work; it's *will you join* the 3.5 percent?

PART III
Lighting the Way Forward

Once we understand our power and the personal and collective benefits of using it, the only question left is *how* to use it. This final section is about your own engagement, the demonstration of *your* hope through *your* action.

We begin by asking, "Where Do We Go From Here?" Two futures are before us. One asks nothing of us and leads toward decline. A second demands far more but offers hope.

Here, we also explore the two types of action citizens take to ensure democracy and how ordinary people sustain the momentum democracy needs. "Effecting and Sustaining Change" shows that citizens are already building a bulwark against tyranny. It helps to know that we aren't alone, that stalwarts have been busy already.

Then comes "Light Many Fires," meant to help you find yourself in democratic action. No one movement or leader will save us or guarantee democracy; renewal will come from countless small acts. When each of us lights a candle, a torch, or a bonfire of courage, the light will spread as we work together, conversation by conversation, project by project, neighborhood by neighborhood.

This last section is not a curtain fall, but the opening act of a great renewal. The hero returns home changed, ready to serve. What began in exhaustion ends in renewed vitality. The message is as simple and old as liberty itself: When *We the People lead, the leaders will follow.*

8

Where Do We Go From Here?

We get a dire future if we do nothing. A more desirable one requires all of us to stand up.

There are times in a nation's life when the path forward is no longer a matter of routine politics but requires choosing between fundamentally different futures. America is in such a moment.

The tensions described in earlier chapters—the rise of Christian nationalism, the erosion of pluralism, the disengagement of millions, and widespread spiritual distress—are not passing storms. They are converging forces reshaping the country for the worse.

At present, a passionate right-wing minority holds significant structural advantages. It benefits from a president in the Oval Office, control of both chambers of Congress, a sympathetic Supreme Court, and a conservative media ecosystem that continually reinforces its worldview. The design of our political system further amplifies this influence through the Electoral College, equal representation in the Senate, and the disproportionate power of smaller, more homogeneously conservative states.

Opposing this—but only passively—is the Exhausted Majority: a broad, diverse, pluralistic, and individualistic public that still believes in freedom, fairness, and democratic norms, yet remains scattered, overwhelmed, and difficult to mobilize. They—we—are not yet acting as a political force. Our future depends on whether we step forward.

This conflict reflects a clash of aspirations about what America is and what it should become. Unless the Exhausted Majority moves from the sidelines into public life, however, the outcome will not be decided by persuasion or consensus. It will unfold as a long struggle shaped by imbalance, resentment, and rising instability. The stakes are nothing less than whether the United States remains a pluralistic democracy—or slides toward something narrower, harsher, and spiritually diminished.

Two outcomes are possible. Neither is preordained. One comes to pass if the Exhausted Majority stays on the sidelines. Only one, the harder path, offers hope.

FUTURE ONE: PROLONGED INFIGHTING

In this future, the extreme right either consolidates power—what it fervently wants—or responds to electoral defeat with escalating destabilization. Either way, the outcome is easy to see. In this future, Trump is succeeded by J.D. Vance or a similar figure cut from the same cloth or by a liberal president like Gavin Newsom, Josh Shapiro, or J.D. Pritzker whose legitimacy is rejected by a radicalized minority. Congress, already weakened, slips into near-total paralysis. Governance gives way to permanent crisis. Government shutdowns become routine symptoms of institutional breakdown rather than extraordinary events. Agencies responsible for elections, justice, food and drug safety, and scientific research struggle to function as budgets, appointments, and authorizations stall indefinitely.

Exhausted by ceaseless rancor and convinced participation no longer matters, growing numbers of exhausted Americans retreat further from civic life. The withdrawal is not ideological but psychological—an act of self-preservation. That retreat spreads to the nation's intellectual and creative classes. Scientists, medical researchers, technologists, policy thinkers, and artists—especially the young—look abroad for stability, funding, and freedom from political interference. Those who cannot leave physically withdraw inward. Anger hardens. Resentment gathers. America's reputation as a beacon of democracy and a pulsing center of innovation dims, then fades away.

As instability deepens, cultural and constitutional guardrails weaken. Press freedoms narrow. Academic independence, already threatened, continues to erode as universities face ideological litmus tests tied to funding and accreditation. Civil liberties contract.

A narrow and distorted version of Christianity increasingly seeps into law and public policy, redefining "American" in exclusionary terms. The separation of church and state—long a cornerstone of religious freedom and pluralism—frays, then effectively collapses.

Election administration, once professional and nonpartisan, becomes openly politicized. Competing factions claim fraud in any contest they lose. Trust in electoral legitimacy disintegrates, leaving millions convinced that elections are neither free nor fair. Democracy becomes procedural theater without shared belief in outcomes.

The fractures appear first not in Washington, but in living rooms. Families already strained by years of suspicion begin to pull apart. Holiday gatherings shrink. Adult children decline invitations rather than expose themselves—or their children— to ideological tirades. Siblings who once sparred harmlessly now avoid one another entirely, convinced the other side has abandoned basic decency.

Communities follow the same trajectory. School boards, libraries, and town councils become battlegrounds marked by threats, walkouts, and recalls. Teachers, librarians, and local officials—the civic glue of small places—are harassed or forced out for refusing to toe ideological lines. Civic engagement, already at historic lows, falls further as ordinary people withdraw, leaving public life dominated by the angriest and most extreme voices.

Meanwhile, AI-driven media ecosystems amplify every fracture. Misinformation spreads faster than it can be corrected. Trust erodes further. Politics becomes a permanent emergency, drawing even previously disengaged members of the Exhausted Majority into cycles of outrage and fear. Polarization accelerates—not always erupting into open conflict but steadily draining the nation's vitality.

Talk of "soft secession" grows. States aligned with MAGA and Christian nationalist movements begin behaving as semi-autonomous entities, resisting federal authority and asserting parallel legal regimes. Once-fringe calls for national breakup enter mainstream discourse. Political violence—assassinations of judges, politicians, and public officials—shifts from shocking exception to grim recurrence.

At the same time, clusters of states form interstate compacts around climate policy, reproductive rights, public health, and gun laws, creating a patchwork of mini-federations. Citizens vote with their feet, relocating to states that reflect their values. National cohesion weakens further as Americans increasingly live within ideological enclaves rather than a shared civic project.

What I'm describing is not a single dramatic collapse, but a prolonged unraveling: a nation still formally intact, still wealthy and powerful—but hollowed out, brittle, and no longer confident in the idea of *We the People*.

FUTURE TWO: DEMOCRATIC RESILIENCE, THE HARDER PATH

In this scenario, the more difficult choice but the one that ultimately delivers the way of life most of us want, we the Exhausted Majority—today largely silent, scattered, and demoralized—finally steps off the sidelines. This vast multicultural and multiracial majority, one that believes in pluralism, fairness, racial equity, and shared dignity, begins to find its voice. What once felt like resignation becomes resolve. Citizens who had once tuned out rediscover that democracy is not a spectator sport and that their absence has consequences they don't like.

Those who choose to get on this path should be heartened by one fact: We have a tailwind working for us the far-right lacks. For all its fervor and discipline, the movement working against democracy—Christian nationalism, MAGA, and national conservatism—struggles to embed its preferences across the broader population. Make no mistake: They enjoy tremendous power, but as more Americans call out the dangers this worldview poses, that minority is unlikely to grow and can be turned back.

If we open ourselves to the path of democratic resilience, we welcome, even seek new journalistic, political, and moral leaders: figures who speak with clarity, courage, and moral imagination. In this scenario, they do not mimic the old language of left versus right and are not delivering focus-group derived "messages," but instead tell a fresh story about how freedom and responsibility, morality and politics, belong together. These leaders help us redefine and re-own patriotism itself.

In this scenario, new leaders expose the contradictions and cruelties of the far-right while calling us back to the country we aspire to be. Their examples inspire millions of ordinary Americans to take up the humble but transformative work of citizenship—voting with purpose, serving their communities, joining local institutions, organizing neighbor to neighbor, and embracing shared sacrifice. Patriotism, once viewed as stodgy and old fashioned, takes on new resonance and new currency.

This path rises from the ground up as successful democratic movements always have. The story of democracy, briefly hijacked today, is reclaimed in this future by those who believe in it most—the broad American majority. From them, illiberal politicians meet not just resistance but repeated, resounding defeat. The influence of nationalists and nativists fades as the public rejects their vision, and the country's flirtation with authoritarianism comes to an end.

For this to happen, a psychological shift must take place in the minds and hearts of millions of Americans, at least that catalytic 3.5 percent. By this I mean a widespread, unmistakable realization: *We are losing something we value, and no one else is coming to save us.* The shift begins when ordinary people decide, "I can't wait for others to fix the country. I have to step up. I have to take responsibility. This is what being a citizen means."

Such an awakening will almost certainly come along with a rethinking of the role we have allowed consumerism to play in our lives. This is a reassessment already underway among many young Americans. It means questioning the stories we've been sold about what gives meaning to our lives, and what constitutes success, security, and happiness. It means recognizing how the pursuit of *more* has crowded out our connection to one another and weakened the habits of citizenship.

Some social philosophers have used terms like "The Great Turning," "The Third Reconstruction," or "The Long Awakening" to suggest that our country is on the verge of a sweeping social and spiritual reformation. Perhaps what I am describing is what they're referring to. In any case, without something like this, democracy—and perhaps civility itself—is almost certainly lost.

Christian nationalists would tell us that their brand of religion will cure our waywardness, but even if the rest of us succeed in putting that dark movement in its place, we are still left with a spiritual void we must somehow address, most easily seen in the current epidemic of loneliness, anxiety, and high rates of deaths of despair.

I am not arguing here for a revival or for "that old time religion." I'm simply observing a truth: Democratic renewal will require something deeper than institutional fixes, better politicians, better policy, and better messaging. It will require a transformation in how people see themselves and one another, a rethinking of what we owe one another, a reweaving of the moral fabric that binds us. This kind of thinking goes far beyond a debate about the relative merits of AI or any specific environmental proposal, as important as those things are. It goes to the heart of citizenship itself: who we are as a people and what each of us owe to our common life.

America's most important turning points have been accompanied by such moral reorientations: the awakening of conscience that fueled abolition and women's suffrage, the surge of solidarity that underwrote the New Deal, the moral bravery of the civil rights era. Each was propelled not only by new kinds of activists and leaders but by ordinary people who grew tired of the stories they'd been living within and dared to imagine a different one.

In this moment, our task is to cultivate a shared civic, moral, and spiritual imagination vigorous enough not only to withstand divisive forces but also to inspire renewed commitment to the common good. This work asks us to rediscover a spirit of reverence—not in a religious sense, but a genuine respect—for the dignity of others and for the self-worth we nurture by joining together in pursuit of pluralism.

What comes next will be shaped by those willing to step forward, to step out and stand up without any guarantee of victory. That has always been the way of freedom and the promise of America. The question before us is unavoidable: Which future will *We the People* build?

STEPPING INTO YOUR POWER

As I wrote the first scenario above, I found my anxiety rising. Yours may have, too, as you read it. If so, that's a good sign. It means you understand what's at stake.

I wrote this book because there came a moment when something became clear for me. The things I value most—freedom and liberty—are not abstract ideals; they give me my very life. And they are now profoundly threatened. I began to see that feeling concerned was not enough. I needed a plan and I had to decide about how to show up on behalf of my values. Action became necessary—not because action guarantees success, but because inaction guarantees loss.

Here is the truth: Concern is not enough. Understanding isn't enough. Neither is outrage. The future won't be decided by the people who comprehend a threat or who shout about the falling sky. It will be decided by the people who show up to ensure a future that they want for themselves and those they love.

The truth is both fortifying and liberating: Democracy is not easy. It has always turned on the actions of committed minorities, small groups of people who chose courage over comfort and responsibility over resignation.

The extremists drawing on Christian nationalism understand this. And they are counting on the Exhausted Majority to do nothing—for *you and me* to do nothing. Meanwhile, they are organized, disciplined, and relentless.

But then, so were the abolitionists, the suffragists, the civil-rights workers, the democracy reformers, and the countless unnamed citizens who have pushed America closer to its promise in all eras. Hear this: You stand in that lineage. You are not too small, too late, or too alone. The only question is whether you will decide to join with others and act on behalf of your deepest yearnings.

In the next two chapters, we learn how ordinary citizens are cultivating resilience, reclaiming agency, and rebuilding the habits that make democracy work. The most important work doesn't begin in Washington, but in our neighborhoods and daily choices. This is where the future is made.

KEY IDEAS IN THIS CHAPTER

* America is at a crossroads: We face a choice between fundamentally different futures, driven by opposing forces.

* One path leads to national decline: Authoritarian consolidation and cultural narrowing, and prolonged infighting marked by paralysis, fragmentation, and rising violence.

* A second path—Democratic Resilience—offers hope: It depends on millions stepping off the sidelines, rediscovering agency, and reclaiming democracy as a shared responsibility.

* Renewal requires a moral and cultural awakening: Citizens must rethink the Consumer story, deepen their sense of belonging, and develop a civic and spiritual imagination strong enough to counter division.

* History reminds us that committed, courageous minorities have always shaped America's direction.

9

Politics ought to be the part-time profession of every citizen.

—DWIGHT DAVID EISENHOWER

The people are the rightful masters of both Congress and the courts, not to overthrow the Constitution but to overthrow the men who pervert the Constitution.

—ABRAHAM LINCOLN

Restoring and Sustaining Democracy

We've Faced the Problems, We've Prepared for the Fight, Now We Act

Every era brings its own test of democracy. Our time may not ask us to load muskets, storm beaches, or march across bridges, but it does ask something just as difficult. It asks us to mobilize, become engaged, and stay hopeful in a time when we are rewarded for cynicism and flight.

It helps to know that across the country, increasing numbers of citizens are finding new ways to stand up for democracy.

In increasing numbers, ordinary Americans are seeing the hypocrisy in our politics, are disgusted with vast sums of money that are distorting it, and are pushing back. Some are defending voting rights in courtrooms; others are organizing local rallies to remind us that no person—no king—stands above the law. Journalists, teachers, and neighbors are pushing back against disinformation and despair. Each act may seem small, but together they become a great chorus of renewal, a living proof that self-government still breathes, still struggles, still sings.

This chapter is meant not only to reassure you that democracy's defenders are active. It's also meant to help you find your place among them. Our moment may feel precarious, but it is also alive with possibility. History tips according to the choices people make—people like you.

In this chapter, I'll introduce two kinds of actions citizens must take—one type *restores* democracy and the other *sustains* it. Our moment, one in which democracy itself feels under threat, calls more urgently for restoring behaviors than sustaining ones, though both are essential. Throughout our history, from the Revolution to the Progressive Era to the Civil Rights and Vietnam years, Americans have taken both kinds of action, rebuilding what was broken and sustaining what keeps community vital. To use metaphors, when democracy is wounded, citizens must become *fighters and healers*; when it is healthy, we must be *shepherds and gardeners*.

Before we go too far, let me offer a way to think about choosing where and how to get involved. In an interview, columnist David French reflected on the question he's often asked by people anxious about our beleaguered democracy: "What can

I do?" He acknowledged there's no single answer, but he shared a story. Growing up in the South, he often wondered what his own relatives had done during the Civil Rights Movement. Did they stand for justice, stay silent, oppose it, or choose some other path? He urges people today to ask themselves a similar question: When future generations look back, what would you want them to learn about what *you* did when democracy was under threat? That, he says, is where your answer lies.

Democracy-Restoring Activities

Actions in this category are often highly visible initiatives citizens take when democratic norms, institutions, or shared truths have eroded. These are efforts aimed at *repair and renewal*. These include organizing resistance to antidemocratic forces, defending voting rights, rebuilding trust across divides, mobilizing for accountability, and reasserting civic values in public life. Later, I will give you many examples of organizations that are taking actions like this. Consider joining them.

Restoring behaviors are *corrective*. These are assertive, often confrontative actions that seek to bring about change needed to get democratic practices back into alignment with its principles. Restorative activities are meant to generate feelings; camaraderie and hope on the part of the resisters, discomfort on the part of the parties and institutions being resisted.

Citizens take restorative actions when the system falters. As Erica Chenoweth's research shows, the most effective of these are nonviolent, though they are anything but passive. Restorative activities channel frustration and anxiety into courage, solidarity, and moral pressure.

Democracy-Sustaining Activities

These actions, covered in the next chapter, keep democracy healthy once it is functioning. These are efforts aimed at *maintenance and stewardship*. These include voting, volunteering, participating in local governance, joining associations, mentoring youth, supporting journalism, and nurturing habits of dialogue and compromise. Sustaining behaviors are generative. They keep the civic ecosystem vibrant and resilient over time.

POWERFUL EFFORTS ARE ALREADY UNDERWAY

In this section, I highlight organizations confronting the forces that threaten our democracy. Each one addresses a specific "dark force"—political extremism, civic decline, oligarchy, or the mental and spiritual health crisis. Not all of these organizations function as traditional grassroots movements with local chapters. Even so, they play a vital role as sources of knowledge and awareness, equipping individuals, civic groups, and institutions with tools, data, and narrative frameworks that strengthen democratic engagement.

As you read about each effort, consider the ways you can get involved. If there is a petition to sign, this is the easiest way to show your support, but in this perilous moment, each of us must find ways to do more than this. And consider donating. Even small amounts help. Here are some possibilities:

* Join locally. Connect with a state or community chapter and get involved.
* Show up. Attend trainings, town halls, or workshops; volunteer to help organize or facilitate.

- ✴ **Educate others.** Use available tool kits and reports to lead discussions in schools, congregations, or neighborhoods.
- ✴ **Speak out.** Contact legislators, sign petitions, or write letters and op-eds to defend democracy.
- ✴ **Create space.** Start or host a discussion circle or civic club if none exist.
- ✴ **Share widely.** Circulate trusted resources to inform and inspire others.

EFFORTS FOCUSING ON COMBATTING POLITICAL EXTREMISM

Common Cause is a nonpartisan, grassroots organization working to make government more open, accountable, and responsive to the people. It serves as a citizens' lobby for democracy by advocating for fair elections, voting rights, campaign-finance reform, an end to gerrymandering, and ethical standards in government. Through litigation, public education, and organizing, Common Cause empowers Americans to hold power to account and strengthen democratic institutions at every level, from city halls to Congress.

Today, Common Cause is focused on confronting the most urgent threats to democratic governance. It is working to protect election administrators from harassment, challenge partisan power grabs in state legislatures, and push for transparency around AI-generated political content. Its state chapters mobilize volunteers as nonpartisan poll monitors, advocate for independent redistricting commissions, and fight efforts to restrict ballot access. Nationally, Common Cause continues to champion reforms like the Freedom to Vote Act and the John

Lewis Voting Rights Advancement Act, ensuring that the rules of our democracy serve the people, not the powerful.

Southern Poverty Law Center (SPLC) is a nonprofit legal advocacy and education organization dedicated to fighting hate, teaching tolerance, and seeking justice for the most vulnerable. The organization is best known for tracking and exposing extremist and hate groups through its *Intelligence Project* and *Hate Map*, while also pursuing civil rights litigation to protect marginalized communities. SPLC works to dismantle systems of oppression through legal action, public education, and partnerships that advance racial equity and democracy.

Today, the SPLC is deeply engaged in monitoring the surge of extremist activity, documenting threats to election workers, and exposing networks that spread conspiracy theories and political violence. Through strategic litigation, it challenges discriminatory laws, protects immigrant and LGBTQ+ communities, and holds hate groups legally accountable for intimidation and harm. SPLC also invests heavily in education, providing schools and communities with tools to counter radicalization and build cultures of inclusion, strengthening the civic foundations that extremism seeks to erode.

Braver Angels is a nonpartisan, nationwide nonprofit dedicated to bringing Americans together across political divides. Its programs intentionally pair people who lean left with those who lean right to reduce polarization and strengthen democratic culture. Through sophisticated—and often free—workshops, structured debates, and facilitated dialogues, Braver Angels teaches practical skills for listening and disagreeing constructively. Local alliances convene citizens from diverse ideological backgrounds to build understanding and a shared sense of civic purpose. Participants can even sign up for a one-on-one conversation with someone whose politics differ from their own, practicing what the organization calls "disagreeing better."

Today, Braver Angels is expanding its reach as polarization intensifies. The organization now trains community leaders, faith groups, and even state legislators in depolarization skills, and its Red-Blue workshops are held in hundreds of communities nationwide. It produces public debates on contentious issues, offers online skills courses, and mobilizes volunteers to bring respectful dialogue into schools and local civic spaces. Increasingly, Braver Angels is partnering with universities, libraries, and local governments to embed the practice of "disagreeing better" into the civic life of communities that are struggling to stay connected.

CACN is a nationwide, faith-based movement that equips Christians to recognize, resist, and respond to the dangers of Christian nationalism. CACN brings together people of many denominations to defend religious freedom, promote pluralism, and strengthen democracy through faith-rooted action and education. The organization provides practical tools such as discussion guides, videos, fact sheets, sermon materials, and event templates, to help individuals and congregations engage this issue in their own communities.

Democracy Docket is a digital news and analysis platform founded in 2020 that focuses on tracking, reporting on, and interpreting litigation, legislation, and administrative actions related to U.S. voting rights and elections. The site publishes free daily and weekly newsletters, maintains a detailed database of court cases and election-law developments, and offers insightful opinion pieces and long-form interviews with leading voices in the democracy and legal-rights community. A companion law firm litigates voting and election cases and has done so in over 30 states.

EFFORTS FOCUSING ON OLIGARCHY

Democracy Fund, on its website, says it "is a foundation working to build an inclusive, multiracial democracy that is open, just, resilient, and trustworthy." Created by eBay founder and philanthropist Pierre Omidyar, Democracy Fund and its partner organization Democracy Fund Voice have together committed over $500 million in grants since 2014 to support those working to strengthen democracy. Consider donating, subscribing to their blogs or newsletters to follow where they're directing attention, and sharing their reports and insights with your network (religious groups, community orgs, book clubs) to help raise awareness of democratic issues.

Issue One is a nonpartisan reform organization dedicated to reducing the influence of big money in politics and strengthening the integrity of American democracy. It works to curb corruption, protect elections, and increase government accountability through policy advocacy, bipartisan coalitions, and investigative reporting. Its programs build bridges across party lines to advance campaign-finance reform and ethical governance.

The Brennan Center for Justice is a nonpartisan law and policy institute working to strengthen democracy, protect voting rights, and ensure equal justice. It combines rigorous research, public advocacy, and litigation to defend fair elections, reform campaign finance, and promote government transparency. The Center's experts frequently testify before Congress and provide trusted, data-driven analysis to policymakers, journalists, and the public.

EFFORTS FOCUSING ON CIVIC DECLINE AND MENTAL HEALTH

National Conference on Citizenship is a nonpartisan nonprofit dedicated to strengthening civic life in America. It tracks and measures civic health via its *Civic Health Initiative*, publishes the *Civic Health Index*, and convenes stakeholders around civic-engagement trends and community capacity building. It targets the underlying structural issue of diminishing civic participation, social trust, and associational life. The organization's Algorithmic Transparency Institute (ATI) is focused on bringing greater transparency to the digital platforms that impact civic discourse, furthering understanding of the role of digital media on society and our democracy.

The Civic Health Initiative leads National Conference on Citizenship's (NCoC) capacity-building work, in which the organization consults with or convenes state civic coalitions, local community foundations, and regional civic collaboratives. A typical project involves creating a multi year civic health strategy for a city or region, helping local leaders use data to strengthen volunteer pipelines, neighborhood associations, and community problem-solving networks. This work is highly hands-on, often involving stakeholder convenings, data analysis, pilot programs, and implementation design.

Points of Light is one of the world's largest organizations dedicated to volunteerism and civic engagement. Founded by President George H. W. Bush in 1990, it mobilizes millions of volunteers globally through a network of local affiliates, corporations, and nonprofits. Its mission is to inspire, equip, and connect people to take action that improves their communities, thus helping bridge social divides and strengthen democratic participation through service. Points of Light provides resources for individuals, companies, and communities to design and sustain meaningful volunteer programs that address local needs while building civic pride and connection.

The American Foundation for Suicide Prevention (AFSP) is the leading U.S. nonprofit dedicated to saving lives and bringing hope to those affected by suicide. AFSP funds cutting-edge research, advocates for public policies that support mental health, and provides educational programs that raise awareness about suicide prevention and reduce stigma. The organization operates through a network of local chapters in all 50 states, connecting survivors, advocates, and community members to resources that foster connection and resilience.

Weave: The Social Fabric Project addresses the widespread decline of social trust in the United States by connecting, equipping and investing in "weavers," local leaders who foster belonging, relationship, and inclusive community life. Founded in 2018, Weave supports those working quietly in neighborhoods across the country by offering training, micro-grants, peer networks, story-sharing platforms, and a national speakers bureau. It partners with communities to build hubs of trust, convene gatherings, and elevate everyday acts of neighborliness so that the fabric of civic life is strengthened and a culture of connection replaces isolation and division.

Weave's work takes many forms, but two projects capture its core mission. Both projects demonstrate Weave's approach:

lifting up local leaders, equipping them with tools and small resources, and cultivating spaces where connection can replace the isolation and division fraying civic life. In one initiative, Weave partners with a local community foundation to create a Weave hub, a place where neighborhood leaders receive training in relationship-building, small grants to support acts of neighborliness, and regular peer-learning sessions that help them strengthen trust across lines of difference. In another project, Weave collaborates with a city library system to host a series of community storytelling gatherings, where residents share personal experiences, learn facilitation skills, and begin launching their own micro-projects ranging from block-level mutual-aid circles to youth mentorship efforts that weave people together.

STEPPING INTO YOUR POWER

By now, you've seen that meaningful change isn't dramatic or instant; it's steady, relational, and cumulative. Your power lies in finding a rhythm you can maintain: voting in every election, joining a local chapter of a national organization, reading research articles. Democracy is strengthened not by bursts of passion but by patterns of engagement. What matters is not how much you do at one time or even how much you donate but how steadily you keep showing up, keep working with others to achieve things.

Across the country, initiatives to defend and strengthen democracy are already underway, but they need each of us to use the knowledge they've gained, and they need our financial support. All of these organizations are fighting daily in courtrooms, legislatures, and communities to ensure fair elections, protect voting rights, uphold the rule of law, strengthen communities, and promote mental health. Their staff and organizers are pushing back against disinformation, gerrymandering, and authoritarian tactics, but they can't do it alone. Democracy is not self-executing; it survives only when *We the people* step forward to defend it.

In the final chapter, we turn to what it means to light many fires of hope and rebirth—sustaining activities that individuals can take that have the potential to spread across neighborhoods, cities, and our country.

Key Ideas in This Chapter

* Every era tests democracy; ours demands courage, engagement, and hope over cynicism and flight.
* Democracy's renewal depends on two kinds of action: restoring (repairing what's broken) and sustaining (nurturing what endures).
* Big movements grow from small, local efforts—churches, schools, and neighbors weaving the fabric of renewal.
* Significant efforts to defend and strengthen democracy are already underway, but all of us must lend our support—our time, our voice, and our resources—to sustain them.

10

At some level, the path forward is simple: Treat people with respect, truly care for others, do the right thing regardless of the circumstances, have a servant heart, think less of yourself and more of others. Then, watch what happens.

—TODD CORNWELL, CHURCH MINISTRY DIRECTOR

Light Many Fires

Reclaiming Your Power to Build Community and Effect Change By Getting Involved—Your Way

Right now, in every town and neighborhood, people in large numbers are quietly caring for someone or something they love—helping a neighbor, mentoring a child, repairing what's broken. Beneath the ache and heartbreak about how things are going in our country lies a beautiful fact: The instinct of Americans is to care and they show it every day. I see it everywhere and all day long, in big acts and small. I see it at the gym when someone leaves a water bottle behind and another gym rat scurries to return it. I saw it an hour ago when my neighbor helped another neighbor change the wiper blades on his car.

The question before us in today's America, though, is not whether we care, but whether we can coalesce our caring into shared purpose, whether we can kindle our individual sparks into a common flame bright enough to guide a country that desperately needs its light.

Many want change but are discouraged. The problems seem so big, but I am so small. For those who are still skeptical that you can make a difference, I have a story from 1966 that might encourage you. It concerns a speech given by Robert F. Kennedy, then a senator, to a group of young, white antiapartheid activists in Cape Town, South Africa. The country was in the grip of apartheid; the efforts of these young people were thwarted at every turn. They were taking a risk to even be in the room. Kennedy's job was to encourage them, a daunting task.

In the speech, Kennedy challenged his young audience to reject fear and passivity and to see themselves as agents of moral change. His words are among the most quoted lines of his career and assure all who read them that if we do *anything* to help others or stand for a principle, or do something to bring people together, it counts. Kennedy said:

> Each time a man [or woman] stands up for an ideal, or acts to improve the lot of others, or strikes out against injustice, he [or she] sends forth a tiny ripple of hope, and crossing each other from a million different centers of energy and daring, those ripples build a current which can sweep down the mightiest walls of oppression and resistance.

Kennedy was encouraging continuing activism and by telling them their calling is not just one of politics but the work of conscience and ethics. They had, therefore, the most powerful force in the universe behind them: moral authority. In dark times, we need to remind ourselves that anything we might do, if it comes from a sincere interest in the well-being of a neighborhood, community, or country, comes from this same source of power.

In the last analysis, it's up to us as individual Americans to ensure a hopeful future. Collective action is necessary, but this means each of us must take a step first. We must join in. We do so by voting, by helping our neighbors, by serving meals at a homeless shelter, by making our voices heard, by putting our effort and/or our dollars behind some initiative. All of this may sound daunting if you've never volunteered anywhere or feel isolated, but here's the comforting truth: Doing just about *anything* to make one's world—one's neighborhood, city, or country—a better place reduces personal stress. It also supports the basic necessity of both mental health and democracy, namely, social connectedness.

When we take an action of constructive engagement, even a very small act like joining with others to clean up a vacant lot or volunteering for an hour at the library, the world—both our inner world and our outer world—gets better. Then, when we act in concert with others to enhance community life or do something to make our system of government stronger, we multiply our power. And it gets better yet: As we do these things, we reduce a second problem—social isolation.

This chapter is about how to make a difference through those democracy-sustaining activities that anyone can take.

But before we get too far, I want to beg you *not* to try to change the world, at least not by yourself. Instead, join with others and contribute something to your neighborhood or community first. Don't get carried away; stay local, stay modest. Then, as you acquire a taste for activism, by all means, go on to bigger things.

My friends Jan and Rachel are staying local. When Trump got reelected and issued many executive orders on his first day in office designed to offend Democrats like them, they were discouraged briefly. But they got quickly into action.

They invited twenty friends and neighbors to Rachel's home for a potluck dinner. If it had ended there, it would already have been a success. But after sharing the meal, we gathered in the small living room and shared how we felt about our country, a conversation that proved unexpectedly cathartic. Wearing "We the People" T-shirts, they spoke of their purpose, which was to help one another do what we can to stand up for democracy. The group is still meeting monthly, encouraging individual and collective action. I doubt I would have written this book without their influence, and I remain deeply grateful.

Matthew told me: "I volunteer once a week at a local food cupboard, assisting people in picking out food for their families. It is very gratifying to give people those moments where someone just related to them human-to-human to help them get things done."

This chapter encourages action, but please be clear: You don't have to get into politics to improve your neighborhood or our country. Some of us gravitate to political activism, but most of us don't. That's just fine. I repeat: Doing anything to help improve things counts!

My aim in this chapter is to help you find *your* way, respecting *your* time and other limitations. I begin by helping you decide how much of a commitment to make. Then, I offer some guidance about how to use your gifts to join with others in making your part of the world a bit better or, if this is more your style, joining a movement to fight the good fight.

> Kerrie loves to sing. When a relative was in hospice, a singing group came and provided comfort to the patient and the family. She since joined the group and feels deep fulfillment from it. I got her to tell me about what it feels like to sing for people who are dying. As she spoke, a visible contentment came over her, a beautiful peace.

GUIDELINES

Let's start with some rules of thumb.

Join something—anything. The guideline here is simple: Be with people and join in their activities. As we've been exploring in this book, the share of Americans saying they belong to any club, group, union, church, service group, neighborhood group, or association of any sort has dropped steadily and significantly over the last twenty years. We've explored the effects of this on mental health and democracy.

Only get involved in things that nourish you! If I had a magic wand, I'd wave it over every neighborhood and town, every suburb and urban area, and it would result in people coming out of their homes, away from their TVs and social media and news feeds and into conversations with their neighbors, into helping their neighbors, into joining things, into working with others in a cooperative way. But my magic wand would also prevent any person from taking action that depleted them or took them away from caring for themselves or their families or tending to a responsibility. Take care of yourself, the old saying goes, so you can take care of others. And remember: It is no sin to get involved only in things that nourish *you*. Make it a win-win.

Start locally and modestly. Don't think about fixing all of America. Instead, think about doing something to improve your block, your neighborhood, or your kid's school. Americans learn democracy by practicing it in small spaces first. Join your neighborhood association, volunteer at the local library, coach Little League, help organize a community garden, or start a neighborhood tool lending system. Burnout serves no one. Sustainable engagement beats heroic exhaustion. Start smaller than you think you can handle—you can always increase involvement as you go.

Rhonda, who cuts my hair, brought tears to my eyes when she told me about the time when her son was doing drugs and was homeless. She couldn't get him to come home even for a meal. But he would allow her to be with him as she gave haircuts to his homeless friends. She brought sandwiches when she did.

Show up consistently. The magic in those service organizations—Lions, Rotary, Kiwanis, etc.—if there is any, isn't in rituals or the creeds but in the regularity of the people who keep coming to the monthly meetings, who stay after to stack chairs, who remember names and ask about people's kids. Social capital builds through repeated, face-to-face interactions over time.

Bridge differences instead of avoiding them. Look for opportunities to work alongside people who don't share your politics but do share your concern for the neighborhood school or local park. The strongest communities Alexis de Tocqueville observed brought together people who disagreed about some things but found common ground in others.

Make it about doing, not talking. Instead of complaining about the troubles in our country or some politician's latest outrage, work with others on projects with tangible outcomes—cleaning up a local stream, mentoring kids, helping elderly neighbors with groceries, pitching in at the food pantry. Sharing work builds trust. Ranting about politics doesn't.

Denise told me, "My son with Asperger's and I deliver Meals on Wheels to clients every Wednesday to people whose families live far away from them. The people we deliver to have begun to think of us as their local family and they look forward to seeing my son, especially. He has a beautiful smile. Everyone delights when he comes." Needless to say, their delight in her son delights her, too.

WHO IS LIGHTING THE FIRE? AN ACTIVISM READINESS ASSESSMENT

I am going to use the metaphor of flames. I will say that your contribution can be that of a modest candle, a more vigorous torch, or an awesome bonfire. Before you choose *how* to engage in making your neighborhood, town, or our country a better place, do yourself a favor by honestly assessing your capacity to get involved. We're all different, and no level of involvement is insignificant. What matters is not how brightly you burn compared to others but that you contribute your flame to the whole.

CAN YOU LIGHT A CANDLE? (LOW CAPACITY)

You have limited time and energy.
  You might be here if:

* You've never been politically active beyond voting and you don't belong to anything right now.
* You have young children, a demanding job, or health limitations.
* You feel overwhelmed by daily life responsibilities.
* You want to help but don't know where to start.

  Suggested commitment level: one to three hours per month.
  Starting actions to consider: Small donations, one-time volunteer events, taking something to the neighbors who just moved in. (If you do the latter, be sure to include your contact info written down and an offer to be a resource in loaning gardening tools, resourcing plumbers, etc.)

Nonpolitical example: Ann, an environmental advocate, lives in a retirement community. She has been collecting and providing milkweed seeds and starter plants to others in her development to attract monarch butterflies. Doing this puts her in touch with other residents and helps an endangered species. Monarchs, she told me, "are endangered pollinators and a crucial part of the food web. We're seeing many, many more monarchs now. Seeing the caterpillars and monarchs gives me great joy, and I know others are enjoying their beauty too."

Political activism example: George is very concerned about an off-year election of judges in his state. When he noticed that a political party has rented a storefront in his town, he walked in and asked how he might help, explaining that he is not the go door-to-door type and has never gotten involved in politics before. The workers there sent him home with a list of infrequent voters and a stack of postcards. "I could do this without feeling uncomfortable," he told me. He went back twice for more postcards and has learned about other ways he might get involved later.

COULD YOU LIGHT A TORCH? (MEDIUM CAPACITY)

You have moderate availability.
You might be here if:

* You've volunteered occasionally or attended rallies.
* You can carve out regular time but have other priorities.
* You're comfortable with basic organizing activities or have time for an ongoing commitment.
* You want ongoing but manageable involvement.

Your commitment level: four to ten hours per month

Best starting actions: Monthly organizational meetings, regular phone banking, local government attendance, small leadership roles.

Nonpolitical example: Lloyd teaches English as a second language. He meets with the person he's helping every week for two hours. He told me, "It's fulfilling and satisfying because I can see him progress and I truly believe I'm helping." He told me about a student who, at first, was very shy about speaking. Lloyd told me, "I found out that he had been a professional artist in Haiti and started asking him about his work. We began there and moved along to talking with each other about our weekends and house projects. By the end of the term, he was trying to speak at every opportunity."

Maya's efforts to restore a neglected neighborhood park offer another example. She has been organizing weekend clean-ups, planting native shrubs and trees, and partnering with local businesses to sponsor benches, lighting, and playground repairs. By bringing neighbors together, she is turning what began as a shared frustration over litter and safety into a collective effort to create a welcoming public space for families. Her story illustrates how community improvement often starts close to home, with someone deciding that a better, more connected neighborhood is worth the effort.

Political activism example: Every election cycle, Linda reaches out to her local political party and asks how she can best help. She isn't comfortable going door-to-door, so party officials have asked her to do other things that align with her skills as a school administrator. During some cycles, she organizes data and manages phone banks, coordinating volunteer schedules so that every precinct is covered. At other times, she trains new volunteers on how to answer voter questions and keeps track of the flow of materials like sample ballots and campaign literature.

For Linda, the satisfaction comes from putting her organizational skills to use in a way that strengthens the community. She likes knowing that even though she's not on the front lines of canvassing, her behind-the-scenes work ensures that others can succeed. She has built relationships with neighbors and volunteers who share her values, and each election she sees firsthand how her efforts make the local operation run more smoothly.

What keeps her coming back is the sense that she is contributing to something larger than herself. "I may not be knocking on doors," she told me, "but I'm helping open them for others." For Linda, democracy depends not only on those who speak directly with voters but also on the many who quietly keep the machinery of civic life humming.

MIGHT YOU LIGHT A BONFIRE? (HIGH CAPACITY)

You're ready for significant commitment and possibly leadership.
    You might be here if:

* You've been active in causes before or have a big idea about helping your neighborhood or town.
* You have a flexible schedule or can prioritize activism and a big effort.
* You're comfortable speaking publicly and organizing others.
* You're ready to make this a big commitment.

Your commitment level: 10+ hours per month

Nonpolitical example: My friend Nina lit a bonfire that will probably never be the subject of a newspaper or television story but that has made a tremendous difference in my life and the lives of the many others involved. Back in 2020, when George Floyd was murdered by a policeman in Minneapolis and riots broke out, Nina, who is Black, felt very sad, discouraged, and for a time, bitter. But she decided not to give in to those feelings and instead, did something very constructive.

Nina took it upon herself to start a group to discuss, understand, and reduce racial tensions. She reached out to a white friend and they convened a discussion group made up of half Blacks, half whites. I was one of them (I'm white). Every month, via Zoom, this group has an open discussion in a context of loving support where participants share their perceptions, their desires for greater understanding, and explore topics that reveal our common humanity. People from all over the country now join in. After six years, we're still going. Every so often, local members gather for a meal. We have become friends. We pair up—one Black person, one white—and rotate leadership of the group, bringing fresh discussion topics and inviting in speakers. Every time we meet, our respect and appreciation, even love, of one another grows.

My friend Zak has also lit a bonfire. Several years ago, he was nearly crippled by hip pain that progressed until he could no longer walk. During his recovery, he began practicing tai chi, the martial art known for slow, deliberate movements that cultivate balance, strength, and inner calm.

After undergoing surgery and a long recovery, Zak felt a desire to give something back.

Fast forward to today. Now Zak offers six tai chi classes every week, four in person and two online, all free of charge. Each one-hour class draws as many as 20 people. Zak says the participants are so grateful for the experience that they often burst into spontaneous applause at the end. He hastens to explain. "Oh, it's not for me. They're clapping for the community, for what we created together that day." Curious, I went to one of his classes to see for myself. Toward the close of the session, in complete silence and for nearly ten minutes, everyone began moving in unison, a quiet wave of synchronized gestures flowing gracefully across the room and back. Step, pause, breathe, turn. The effect was mesmerizing. The looks on the faces said *We are in this together. We are at peace. We are one.*

I asked Zak how he feels when a class erupts in applause. He smiled and said, "When I hear that, I feel deeply satisfied. I know I'm on my path. I know I've helped create something that matters."

Political activism example: Barbara has spent the last twenty years serving as a Democratic Committee Woman, the kind of neighborly political role that keeps democracy functioning at the ground level. Every four years, her name appears on the ballot and, if elected, she gets to help her party get voters to show up at the polls. For all these years, she has made this contribution alongside a full-time job.

Twice a year, she organizes volunteers to sort and deliver thousands of door hangers, canvasses with local candidates for school board or township supervisor, and makes sure petitions are signed so those candidates can even appear on the ballot. On Election Day, her team is there again—staffing tables, greeting voters, answering questions, and standing watch as poll watchers to ensure the process runs fairly. For Barbara, each vote is sacred.

Her responsibilities don't end when the polls close. Barbara also acts as an informal civic educator, keeping people in her community informed about issues, candidates, and the rules of the process. When one woman worried she couldn't vote because she had to attend a family funeral out of town, Barbara explained emergency ballot procedures and made sure this woman's vote still counted. That mix of nuts-and-bolts organizing and one-on-one care for her neighbors is what defines the role for her.

Asked why she continues, Barbara lights up. "I really, really, really feel like I make a difference," she told me. The work has introduced her to people she never would have met otherwise and deepened her ties across her own neighborhood. She has learned an enormous amount about politics, issues, and candidates, but the greater reward is knowing she's helped others learn. Most tellingly, Barbara told me that, for her, committee work isn't just about winning elections; it's about building a more informed, connected, and resilient community.

A BONFIRE OF HOPE

The country you love is being claimed by those who would trade democracy for dominion and call it patriotism. But they are not the majority. People like you are. Your community has people who need your presence, your skills, your goodwill, and *you need them.* Whether you get involved politically or nonpolitically, or both, you are needed. And the person who will benefit most if you get involved is you.

Rise. Speak. Help your neighbors. Beautify. Support. Organize. Vote. Create. Defend. Build. You don't need permission. You don't need perfection. You don't need to become a martyr or deplete yourself with giving, giving, giving. But you do need to begin. Light a fire. Light many fires. Let them burn in your heart and in your actions. Let them burn in city halls and coffee shops, on front porches and in digital spaces.

When *We the People* lead, the leaders will follow. And when enough of us lead, the tide will turn. The enemies of democracy will fall back. The country will heal. Neighborhoods and communities will be better places to live. And history will remember that when democracy was threatened, the people did not flinch. *You* did not flinch. You lit a fire. You stood up for your neighborhood, for your community, for your country.

EPILOGUE

Light Your Fire

Albert Einstein once said that the distinction between past, present, and future is only a myth; but it's a persistent one. The same could be said of our life as a people. Our past is not gone; it lives within us. Our future is not yet born; it awaits our choices. We dwell in one continuous, unfolding story. What will be our next chapter?

As we learned here, the most pressing danger Americans face today isn't extreme right-wing politics, or a mental health/spiritual crisis, or even oligarchy. Those are battles on the surface. The deeper threat to democracy is quieter but more corrosive. It's cynicism, fatigue, and disengagement, the soft tyranny of believing *nothing I do matters*. When that belief spreads, it pinches off the flame of freedom.

The story of this nation, of this time, can be a story of renewal if each of us is willing to light a candle, raise a torch, or build a bonfire. Only *We the People* can make democracy work, ordinary citizens who wonder if doing anything makes a difference but who decide that they can be counted on.

This book began with a meditation on faith in democracy. Russell Moore, a personal hero, says at the end of his podcast: "Light shines in the darkness, and the darkness has not, will not, and cannot overcome it." This, too, is a statement of faith.

So, as we conclude, I ask you: How will *you* light the darkness? What faith will enable you to light a torch to help others see? What bonfire of courage, creativity, and cooperation will you help build? Will your light shine in a homeless shelter, a town hall, a coffee shop, on a neighbor's front porch, or in the vast digital commons? Above all, will it shine in your own heart?

Let this book be not a farewell, but a benediction, a beginning. May it remind all of us that freedom's fire is not spent but still burns within us. And when it burns bright again, may we will be able to say:

We did not yield. We acted. We the People made the difference.

APPENDIX

What the Exhausted Majority Really Believes

SOURCES:

Unless otherwise noted, these figures are derived from Chapter 6 ("The Exhausted Majority") of the 2018 report by More in Common.

$\approx$ *means "approximately"*

ABORTION

* Prefer a prochoice over a prolife stance on abortion: $\approx$ 66 percent
* Abortion should be legal in all or most cases (vs. 36 percent illegal): 63 percent (Pew Research Center, June 12, 2025) (Only 8 percent say abortion should be illegal in all cases, PRRI 2024.)

RACISM

* Racism is at least somewhat serious in America today: 87 percent (average across the four Exhausted Majority tribes; range 83 percent–96 percent)
* Acts of racism are at least somewhat common today: 82 percent
* White supremacists are a growing threat in the United States: 68 percent
* Oppose the use of race in college admissions decisions: 87 percent

GENDER ISSUES

* Support same-sex marriage: 64 percent
* Accepting transgender people is the moral thing to do: 66 percent
* Problems of sexism are at least somewhat serious: ≈ 75 percent

DEMOCRATIC MALAISE

* Feel pessimistic about the state of U.S. politics: 72 percent
* People they agree with politically should be willing to listen and compromise: 65 percent
* We need to heal as a nation (rather than "defeat the evil within the nation"): 64 percent
* Would rather avoid having arguments in personal life: 84 percent

ECONOMICS

* The economic system unfairly favors powerful interests: 70 percent (Pew)
* The U.S. economy is rigged to advantage the rich and powerful: 69 percent (Ipsos)
* Money and wealth in the United States should be more evenly distributed rather than being concentrated: 63 percent (Gallup)

GUN POLICY (SPECIFIC PROPOSALS)

* Support universal background checks for all sales/transfers: ≈86 percent (*KFF Health News*)
* Require a license/permit from local law enforcement before buying a gun (purchaser licensing): 72 percent support (Johns Hopkins National Survey of Gun Policy, fielded Jan 6–24, 2025). (Bloomberg School of Public Health)
* "Red-flag" (ERPO) laws—family can petition court to temporarily remove guns from someone at risk: 77 percent support. (JHU 2025). (Bloomberg School of Public Health)
* Clinicians should be able to petition for ERPO: 77 percent support. (Bloomberg School of Public Health)
* Law enforcement should be able to petition for ERPO: 76 percent support (JHU 2025). (Bloomberg School of Public Health)
* Ban gun possession for people under a temporary domestic-violence protection order: 82 percent support (JHU 2025). (Bloomberg School of Public Health)

* Require safe gun storage: 74 percent support overall; 62 percent support among gun owners. (Bloomberg School of Public Health)
* Permitless carry (carry a loaded gun in public with no permit): only 24 percent support (i.e., ≈76 percent do not support). (Bloomberg School of Public Health)

NOTES

1. https://hiddentribes.us/
2. Kristen Soltis Anderson, "Politicians Are Polarized. American Voters, Not So Much." (*New York Times*, Aug. 29, 2025).
3. M. P. Florina, S. J. Abrams, and J. C. Pope. *Culture War? The Myth of a Polarized America* (1st ed.). (Pearson Longman, 2005).
4. https://www.cambridge.org/core/journals/perspectives-on-politics/article/abs/testing-theories-of-american-politics-elites-interest-groups-and-average-citizens/62327F513959D0A304D4893B382B992B
5. https://cps.isr.umich.edu/2024/03/11/politicalrage/
6. https://arxiv.org/abs/1608.03656
7. The Economy | Economist/YouGov Poll: November 26 - 29, 2022 Survey report. https://today.yougov.com/economy/articles/44599-economy-economist-yougov-poll-november-26-29-2022
8. https://www.brennancenter.org/our-work/research-reports/voting-rights-restoration-efforts-florida
9. https://redistricting.lls.edu/state/colorado/?cycle=2020&level=Congress&startdate=2022-03-18
10. https://en.wikipedia.org/wiki/2025_Maine_Question_2
11. https://citizensandscholars.org/research/civic-outlook-of-young-adults/
12. https://www.epi.org/blog/growing-inequalities-reflecting-growing-employer-power-have-generated-a-productivity-pay-gap-since-1979-productivity-has-grown-3-5-times-as-much-as-pay-for-the-typical-worker/
13. https://jewishjournal.com/cover_story/362766/this-is-not-the-end-of-the-synagogue/
14. https://ispu.org/report-1-mosque-survey-2020/
15. https://news.harvard.edu/gazette/story/2024/10/generative-ai-embraced-faster-than-internet-pcs/
16. https://jamanetwork.com/journals/jama/article-abstract/2805292

17. https://www.beckershospitalreview.com/quality/public-health/americans-are-overdoing-alone-time/
18. https://www.cdc.gov/nchs/products/databriefs/db362.htm
19. https://www.fool.com/money/research/average-household-debt/
20. https://www.stlouisfed.org/on-the-economy/2024/may/which-us-households-have-credit-card-debt
21. https://www.epi.org/publication/charting-wage-stagnation/
22. https://inequality.org/facts/wealth-inequality
23. https://usafacts.org/articles/who-owns-american-wealth/
24. https://www.rand.org/content/dam/rand/pubs/working_papers/WRA500/WRA516-2/RAND_WRA516-2.pdf
25. Chetty et al., (*JAMA*, 2016)
26. https://www.gavinpublishers.com/article/view/deaths-of-despair-a-major-and-increasing-contributor-to-united-states-deaths
27. https://www.jec.senate.gov/public/_cache/files/0f2d3dba-9fdc-41e5-9bd1-9c13f4204e35/jec-report-deaths-of-despair.pdf?utm
28. Hannah Fingerhut, *"Most Americans Say the U.S. Economic System Is Unfair, but High Earners Differ"* (Pew Research Center, 2020)
29. Paul Piff, D. M. Stancato, S. Côté, et al., "Higher Social Class Predicts Increased Unethical Behavior" (*Proceedings of the National Academy of Sciences*, 2012)
30. Ibid
31. "Most Americans Say They Admire the Rich, Especially the Self-Made" in Pew Research Center (2017).
32. Bernie Sanders. *Fight Oligarchy.*
33. https://www.claremont.org/jd-vance-claremont-statesmanship-award-2025/
34. https://www.nytimes.com/2025/11/03/opinion/jd-vance-blood-and-soil-america.html
35. https://www.pewresearch.org/politics/2017/02/16/4-attitudes-toward-increasing-diversity-in-the-u-s/
36. https://becketfund.org/index/2022-findings/
37. https://www.prri.org/wp-content/uploads/2023/02/PRRI-Jan-2023-Christian-Nationalism-Final.pdf

38. *Separation of Church and Hate*, John Fugelsang
39. http://christiansagainstchristiannationalism.org/
40. https://www.pewresearch.org/2024/04/02/views-on-discrimination-in-our-society/
41. https://news.gallup.com/poll/693893/steady-say-racism-against-black-people-widespread.aspx
42. https://www.theatlantic.com/politics/archive/2025/09/charlie-kirk-spiritual-warfare/684389/
43. https://prri.org/research/a-christian-nation-understanding-the-threat-of-christian-nationalism-to-american-democracy-and-culture/
44. https://www.reuters.com/world/us/americans-believe-harsh-political-rhetoric-is-fueling-violence-reutersipsos-poll-2025-09-16/
45. "The Uneasy Conscience of Christian Nationalism" (*Christianity Today*, Sept/Oct 2024).
46. https://www.psypost.org/perceived-social-breakdown-fuels-desire-for-authoritarian-leaders-new-psychology-study-shows/
47. https://www.reuters.com/world/us/first-us-independent-turnout-tops-democrats-ties-republicans-edison-research-2024-11-06/
48. "Is Gen Z Giving Up on Democracy?" (More in Common (U.S.), May, 2025). https://moreincommonus.com/wp-content/uploads/2025/05/Is-Gen-Z-giving-up-democracy.pdf
49. Ibid.
50. *"Is Gen Z Giving Up on Democracy?"* published by More in Common (U.S.) in May 2025.
51. https://thefulcrum.us/ethics-leadership/millennial-politics
52. https://prri.org/research/views-on-lgbtq-rights-in-all-50-states/
53. https://www.closeup.org/young-americans-views-on-politics-and-political-engagement/
54. https://www.pewresearch.org/politics/2022/06/06/americans-views-of-government-decades-of-distrust-enduring-support-for-its-role/
55. https://iop.harvard.edu/youth-poll/50th-edition-spring-2025

56. https://www.nytimes.com/2025/10/13/opinion/gen-z-conservative-christianity.html

57. https://www.cato.org/blog/young-americans-socialism-too-much-thats-problem-libertarians-must-fix

58. https://projects.propublica.org/nonprofits/organizations/800835023?

ACKNOWLEDGEMENTS

When you write a book, you discover what your support system is truly made of. I'm very happy to say mine is made of love.

Debbie McKnight, Dick Watson, Todd Cornwell, Barbara Guido, and Steve Hughes devoted far more hours to reading the manuscript than I had any right to expect. Each offered exceptionally useful critique and made this a better book.

Erin McKnight designed both a classy cover and elegant interior. Amanda McKnight brought the project to life online by building the website. Thank you.

I'm also deeply grateful to Conor, Debbie B., Jan, Jay, JB, Jerry, Joe, Judy, Lloyd, Mary, Rich, Steve, and Zak who read chapters and shared helpful feedback. Also, to David Brake for helpful guidance.

Many members of the Main Line Unitarian Church community gave me permission to tell their stories, providing living examples of what patriotism looks like when viewed through the lens that matters most: service. I'm deeply appreciative and admire you all.

INDEX

1830s America, 25–29; building
democracy, 26–27; citizens
participation civic life, 28;
practicing democracy
in, 28; religion-driven moral
framework, 28; strength of
Americans, 29
1890–1965 America, 29–33; exploitative
labor conditions, 29; farm-to-city
migration, 30; Gilded Age, 30;
Great Depression, 32; home-front
mobilization, 31; income inequality,
32; social capital curve of, 30;
suburbanization, 32; women's
suffrage movement, 31; WWII
effect, 32
1965 to today America, 33–38; church
attendance fall, 35; "cross-cutting"
relationships, 35; decline of
social capital, 33–38; social
fragmentation, 38–40

abortion rights, voters on, 20
Alexander, Jon, 93, 96
Algorithmic Transparency Institute
(ATI), 161
AI technology, 37–38
America: growing faith in, xvii; past,
25–32; see also *1830s America*;
1890–1965 America; *1965 to today
America*
American billionaires, generosity of,
61–62
American Foundation for Suicide
Prevention, The, 162
American Revolution, 130

Anderson, Kristen Soltis, 9
anxiety, social media and, xxv
Atlantic, 82

Baldwin, James, xxviii
Bannon, Steve, xxii
*Benedict Option: A Strategy for
Christians in a Post-Christian
Nation, The*, 76
Biden, Joe, 38
Bowling Alone, 30, 36–37
brain drain, 145
Braver Angels organization, 158–159
Brennan Center for Justice, 160
Burns, Ken, 100
Bush, George H. W., 161

Carnegie, Andrew, 29
Carson, Rachel, 132
Case, Anne, 56
Case for Christian Nationalism, The, 76
change, small groups creating, 129–135
Christian nationalism, 76–80, 150;
Christian nationalists gaining
power, 84–86; conflicting pluralism,
79; divine and political missions,
fusion of, 77; gaining ground,
80–84; Gen Z and, 115–117
Christians Against Christian
Nationalism (CACN), 159
church attendance fall, 35
citizen role, reclaiming, 101–106
Citizens, 93
citizenship beyond voting, 93;
choice to be a citizen, 91–93;
passive subject, 93

Citizen Story, 98–101; lighting a
bonfire, 105–106; lighting a candle,
103; lighting a torch, 103–105;
power in, 100
civic decline, 24–44; and mental health,
future focus on, 161–163; social
media in, xxiv–xxv
civic disengagement by social
media, 17
civic engagement: in community, 5; in
country, 1
Civic Health Index, 161
Civic Health Initiative, 161
Civil Resistance, 131
Civil Rights Movement, 131
Clean Air Act, 132
Clean Water Act, 132
Closson, David, 77
collective action, 167–168
commercial society, 63
Common Cause organization, 157
community building for change,
165–179; activism readiness
assessment, 172; bridging
differences instead of avoiding
them, 171; collective action, 167;
conscience and ethics works, 167;
constructive engagement, 167;
democracy-sustaining activities,
167; getting involved in things that
nourish you!, 169–170; importance,
xiii–xxvi; joining something—
anything, 169; making it about
doing, not talking, 171; showing up
consistently, 171; starting locally
and modestly, 170
constructive engagement, 167
consumer, 93
Consumer Story, 96–98
Courage Collectives, 133

cynicism, xvii–xviii, 17–18, 24, 39, 65,
114, 153, 164, 181

"deaths of despair," 56
Deaton, Angus, 56
DEI (diversity, equity, and inclusion)
programs, 79
Democracy Docket, 159
Democracy Fund, 160
Democracy in America, 26
democracy, restoring and sustaining,
153–164; American Foundation
for Suicide Prevention, The, 162;
Braver Angels, 158; Brennan
Center for Justice, 160; Christians
Against Christian Nationalism
(CACN), 159; civic decline and
mental health, efforts focusing on,
161–163; Common Cause, 157–158;
correctives, 155; Democracy
Docket, 159; Democracy Fund, 160;
donating, 156; Freedom to Vote
Act, 157; *Hate Map*, 158; *Intelligence
Project*, 158; Issue One, 160; John
Lewis Voting Rights Advancement
Act, 157–158; maintenance and
stewardship, 156; National
Conference on Citizenship, 161;
oligarchy, efforts focusing on,
160–161; organizations role,
156–157; Points of Light, 161–162;
political extremism, combatting,
157–160; Red-Blue workshops,
159; repair and renewal, 155;
restoring activities, 155; Southern
Poverty Law Center, 158; stepping
into power, 163–164; sustaining
activities, 156; Weave: The Social
Fabric Project, 162
democracy-sustaining activities, 167

democratic immune system, 41–42;
civic education, 41; mental health,
41; social capital, 41
democratic resilience, 146–149; harder
path, 146–149; patriotism in, 147;
religious revival, 149; stepping into
power, 149–150
deregulation, 48
devoted conservatives (6%) tribes,
13, 14
Dillard, Anya, 122
Dreher, Rod, 76

easy paths consequences, 141–151;
brain drain, 145; extreme right-
wing victory, 142; national
decline, 141–151; polarization, 145;
prolonged infighting, 143–145,
187; soft secession, 145; for the
young, 147
economy and democracy, 62–64;
capitalistic system and, 64–66;
purpose of economy, 62–63
electronic entertainment, 37
empathy gap, 58
Environmental Movement
(1960s–1970s), 132
Environmental Protection
Agency, 132
Exhausted Majority, 1, 3–22;
disengaged mindset, 4;
ideological agreement, 13–14;
moderates (15%), 12; nature of, 11;
on partisan gerrymandering, 15;
passive liberals (15%), 12; political
alienation feeling, 15; politically
disengaged (26%), 12; reality
about, 14; religious beliefs and,
6; sidelining of, 15–16; on social
issues, 13; traditional liberals

(11%) tribes, 12; turning away from
politics/community life, 6–7;
see also seven tribes
extreme right-wing victory, issues
with, 142
extreme risk protection orders, 20

Facebook, 37
Faith & Freedom Coalition
(FFC), 85
Family Promise organization, 91–92
far-right disparage pluralism, 73
flag, using, xvi
Founders' story, 72
Four-Way Test, 34
Freedom to Vote Act, 157
Fugelsang, John, 86
future possibilities, 141–151; see also
democratic resilience; easy paths
consequences
Future Shock, 37

Galloway, Scott, 16
generational change, 37
Gen Zers, 113–118; appealing to,
120–123; and Christian
nationalism, 115–117;
disengagement of, reasons,
119–120; on politics, 120; on
reshaping economic system, 119;
restless generation, 117; stepping
into power, 123–124; support for
socialism, 117–119; on voting,
113–114
gerrymandering, 17
GI Bill, 32
Gilded Age, 29–30, 52
Gould, Jay, 29
Great Depression, 32
guns purchase/use, ideologies on, 13

Hate Map, 158
Hazony, Yoram, 74
Hidden Tribes study, 7–16; Exhausted
    Majority, 6–13; Republicans versus
    Democrats beliefs, 14; wings, 8
home-front mobilization, 31
homelessness, 92
hope, reason for, 18–20; common-sense
    convictions, 18; electoral choices,
    18–19; stepping into power, 20–21;
    supporting pragmatic solutions,
    19; voters bypassing polarized
    legislatures, 18

ideological agreement, 13–14; among
    Exhausted Majority, 13–14
immigration, ideologies on, 14
income inequality, 32
inheritors, role of, 109–124; see also
    *Gen Zers; young in reclaiming
    democracy*
inner state, 94
Instagram, 37, 40
Intelligence Project, 158
iPhone, 37
Issue One, 160

Jefferson, Thomas, 100
Jobs, Laurene Powell, 62
John Lewis Voting Rights Advancement
    Act, 157–158
Johnson, Mike, 82
join with others, xviii

Kennedy, Robert F., 166–167
King, Martin Luther, Jr., 57, 73, 131
Kirk, Charlie, 34, 71, 116, 121

Labor Movement (early
    1900s–1930s), 132

LGBTQ+ and ecological concerns,
    inheritors role in, 115
liberal progressivism, 71
lighting the fire, 172; activism readiness
    assessment, 172; bonfire of hope,
    178–179; lighting a bonfire (high
    capacity), 175–178; lighting a candle
    (low capacity), 172–173; lighting a
    torch (medium capacity), 173–175;
    nonpolitical, 173, 174, 175–176;
    political activism, 173, 174–175,
    177–179; see also *community
    building for changes*
Lincoln, Abraham, 53
loneliness, 38–39
Looking Out For #1, 97

Madison, James, 60, 75
MAGA enclave, home as, xvi
Mamdani, Zohran, 112, 134
March for Our Lives, 122
Marriage Equality Movement
    (1990s–2015), 133
Mason, Lilliana, 34
McCrummen, Stephanie, 82
mental health, 41; future focus on,
    161–163
minority, tyranny of, 67–88; see also
    Christian nationalism; pluralism
moderates (15%) tribes, 12
money influence in politics, ideologies
    on, 13
*Money, Lies and God: Inside the
    Movement to Destroy American
    Democracy*, 81
*MONEY, LIES, AND GOD: Inside the
    Movement to Destroy American
    Democracy*, 84
Moore, Russell, 83, 181
moral collapse, 6

moral logic of wealth, 57–60; "born-on-third-base" privilege, 58; internalizing failure, 59; self-blame, 59

Murthy, Vivek, 38, 39

Musk, Elon, 61

National Conference on Citizenship, 161

nationalism as enemy of pluralism, 71–76; American South plantars and, 72; far-right disparage pluralism, 73; the Founders' story, 72

Netflix streaming, 37

Newsom, Gavin, 143

NextGen America, 122

Next Gen Come Up, The, 122

Ocasio-Cortez, Alexandria, 63–64

oligarchy economic system, 48; data, 50–51; debt burden, 51; deregulation, 49; future efforts focusing on, 160–161; impeding progress, 54–55; in late 1970s, 48; oligarchy kills (innovation), 53–56; oligarchy kills (people and democracy), 56–57; pre-Civil War South and, 54; social media in, xxiv, xxv

Omidyar, Pierre, 160

organized religion, waning of, 35

passive liberals (15%) tribes, 12

patriotic feeling/expression, xvi

paycheck-to-paycheck, 58

Perception Gap study, 14

philanthrocapitalism, 61

pluralism, 41, 68–70; issues with, 70; liberals infatuated with, 72; making

use of, 69; nationalism as enemy of, 71–76; religious pluralism, 78

Points of Light, 161–162

polarization in America, xxi, 7–8; reality of, 8; in future, 158; ideological or policy positions, 10–11

political extremism: combatting, 157–160; social media in, xxiv–xxv

political involvement as loneliness antidote, 134–135

political life, xxii

politically disengaged (26%) tribes, 12

post-pandemic drift, 135

power lost, reasons, 1–3; disengaged mindset, 4–5; moral collapse, 6; see also *Exhausted Majority*

Pritzker, JB, 143

progressive activists (8%) tribes, 11

Putnam, Robert, 30, 33, 36

racism, ideologies on, 13

Reagan, Ronald, 49

Red-Blue workshops, 159

Reed, Ralph, 84

relationship with country, xxi–xxii; break it option, xxii; "the Disengaged" option, xxii; fractured, xxi; stand up for it option, xxii–xxiii

religious beliefs in shaping perspective on America, 5

religiously unaffiliated youths, 35

religious pluralism, 78

remote work, 40

Ringer, Robert, 97

Rockefeller, John D., 29

Roosevelt, Teddy, 53

same-sex marriage, ideologies on, 13

Sanders, Bernie, 63

Scott, MacKenzie, 62
Separation of Church and Hate, 86
service organizations, benefits, 33
seven tribes, 8–13; see also *Hidden Tribes study*
Shapiro, Josh, 143
Silent Spring, 132
small numbers of people, 125–137; American Revolution, 130; Civil Rights Movement, 130–131; creating change, 129–135; Labor Movement (early 1900s–1930s), 132; Marriage Equality Movement (1990s–2015), 133; particiption in local issues, 126–129; political involvement by, 134–135; stepping into power, 135–137; for transformative political change, 125–137; threshold effect, 130; Women's Suffrage Movement (1848–1920), 131–132
Smith, Adam, 63
Snapchat, 37
social capital, 30–31, 41
social capital decline, 23–45; extremism due to, 23–45; spiritual crisis due to, 23–45; weakening democracy, 23–45
social cohesion, decline in, 30
social fragmentation, 38–40; loneliness, 38–39; "third places," loss of, 40
social isolation, 39
social issues, ideologies on, 13
social media threatening democracy, xxiv; civic decline, xxv–xxvi; oligarchy, xxv, xxvi; political extremism, xxv; spiritual crisis, xxv; spiritual despair, xxv
social media, negative impact of, 16–18; civic disengagement, 17; creating polarization, 16–18

socialism, Gen Zers support for, 117–118
Southern Poverty Law Center, 158
spiritual crisis, xxv, 39; social media in, xxiv–xxv
spiritual despair, xxv, 23–45
stepping into power, 43–44
Stewart, Katherine, 81, 84
Steyer, Tom, 122
stories governments tell, 91–108; after WWII, 96; Citizen Story, 98–101; Consumer Story, 96–98; Subject Story, 94–96; see also *citizenship beyond voting*
Subject Story, 94–96
suburbanization, 32, 37
Swing Left, 134

Thomas, Clarence, 82–83
"third places," loss of, 40
TikTok, 37, 40
time that tries our souls, xxi–xxix
Tocqueville, Alexis de, 25–28, 171
Toffler, Alvin, 37–38
TPUSA (Turning Point USA), 120–122
traditional conservatives (19%) tribes, 12
traditional liberals (11%) tribes, 12
transgenders acceptance, ideologies on, 13
Trump, Donald, xvi, xxii
Trump, Eric, 77
trust metrics to assess community, 41–42; trusting behaviors, 42; trusting intentions, 42; trusting spaces, 42
Twitter, 37
Tyler, Amanda, 79

Under Siege, 77

Vance, J.D., 71–73, 83, 143
Virtue of Nationalism, The, 74

wealth in the hands of few, 47–66;
    Madison's warning, 60–62; as
    perils for democracy, 47–66;
    stepping into power, 64–66; as
    unelected co-governors of the
    republic, 52; see also *moral logic of
    wealth*; *oligarchy economic system*
Weave: The Social Fabric Project, 162
Williams, Daniel, 116
Wolfe, Stephen, 76
women's suffrage movement, 31

Women's Suffrage Movement
    (1848–1920), 131
WWII effect, 32, 96

young in reclaiming democracy,
    109–124; Democratic Socialism, 110;
    education, 112; Gen Zers voting,
    113–114; LGBTQ+ and ecological
    concerns, 115; on socialism, 117–119;
    pluralism valuing by, 114; voting,
    112–115; see also *Gen Zers*

Zoom, 37

ABOUT THE AUTHOR

Richard McKnight is a psychologist, writer, and artist devoted to strengthening democracy and renewing community life. *When We the People Lead* is his call for Americans to reject despair, resist authoritarianism, and rediscover—in one another—the enduring joys and responsibilities of citizenship.

His professional life has spanned coaching, teaching, consulting, and leadership roles in both business and nonprofit organizations.

McKnight is the author of two previous books and has illustrated three volumes of poetry. He is a proud Unitarian Universalist and lives in the Philadelphia area.